NATURE'S
CURIOUS·CREATURES

NATURE'S
CURIOUS·CREATURES

BILL HARRIS

SMITHMARK

A FRIEDMAN GROUP BOOK

This edition published in 1991 by SMITHMARK Publishers Inc.
112 Madison Avenue
New York, New York 10016

ISBN 0-8317-6317-5

NATURE'S CURIOUS CREATURES
was prepared and produced by
Michael Friedman Publishing Group, Inc.
15 West 26th Street
New York, NY 10010

Editor: Sharon Kalman
Art Director: Jeff Batzli
Designer: Lynne Yeamans
Photography Editor: Christopher C. Bain

Typeset by The Interface Group
Color separation by Scantrans Pte Ltd.
Printed and bound in Singapore by Tien Wah Press (Pte) Ltd.

SMITHMARK books are available for bulk purchase for sales promotion and premium use. For details write or telephone the Manager of Special Sales, SMITHMARK Publishers Inc., 112 Madison Avenue, New York, New York 10016. (212) 532-6600.

"To all creatures that creep, swim,

or fly,

Peopling the earth, the waters, and

the sky,

From Rome to Iceland, Paris to

Japan...."

Nicolas Boileau-Despréaux, 1636–1711

✦ CONTENTS ✦

◆ INTRODUCTION ◆

We are not alone. There are more than a million different animals who share our world, from the blue whale, five times bigger than the biggest dinosaur that ever lived, down through the two-inch creature called krill that is the mainstay of its diet, and on down to the one-celled protozoa, which itself comes in more than 30,000 varieties.

The biggest corner of the animal kingdom is filled with bugs. There are about 700,000 different kinds of insects flying or crawling around out there. That doesn't count spiders and their cousins, in a class all by themselves with 35,000 different species, or the 2,000 different kinds of centipedes and 8,000 distinctly different types of millipedes, not even related to the hundred-leggers.

There are about 13,000 different kinds of fish and 3,000 species of creatures known as amphibians that are just as much at home on land as in the water. Add to that 11,000 kinds of birds and 5,000 types of reptiles, and our world gets rather crowded. But don't forget the mammals. There are 4,000 different kinds of those, from the 180-ton blue whales to you and me.

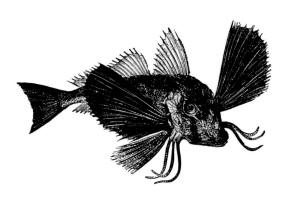

Our
✦ Wildest ✦
Dreams

Every one of the million different creatures running, walking, flying, or swimming through our world has a personality all its own. Some are cute, some are terrifying, but all are fascinating. In spite of this, every culture since the Stone Age has been busy inventing new ones, and even the Bible swears that some of the tales are true. The Book of Job gives a long, detailed description of the leviathan, a creature whose teeth are "terrible round about," and whose airtight scales are joined together so that neither spear nor sword can penetrate them. Sparks of fire come from its mouth and smoke from its nostrils and, according to the biblical account, "Sharp stones are under him: he spreadeth sharp pointed things upon the mire. He maketh the deep boil like a pot." If there ever was such a monster, scientists haven't been able to find any traces of it, and scholars generally write off the description as the result of an encounter with a crocodile.

Alligators and crocodiles are probably also the inspiration for the idea that dragons lurked in every corner of the world, from the court of the emperor of China to caves under medieval castles in Europe. Like the leviathan, no dragon ever left behind any traces of itself, although in some parts of China it's possible to buy dragon bones and eggs, which are said to have magical medical powers. The people who sell them swear they were left behind by creatures who died long ago. The fact is, no one in China would ever dream of killing a dragon if they should happen to run

✦ *William Blake's vision of the behemoth and leviathan was inspired by the Bible.* ✦

into one. The beasts have the power to make it rain to keep the farms productive, but if angered, they can also create floods, which in crowded China have the power to kill hundreds of thousands. Besides, from the very beginning of Chinese history, dragons have been the symbol of the emperor, who was considered to be the son of heaven itself.

In European cultures, dragons were more feared than revered. Rather than being associated with water, they usually breathed fire and, unlike their Oriental counterparts, they often had wings. But the biggest difference between the two cultures was that in Europe, killing one was the greatest act of heroism known to man. Chief among the dragon slayers was St. George, who may never have

become the patron saint of England if he hadn't saved a damsel in distress by dispatching a dragon. According to one version of the story, a princess was next on the list to be sacrificed to the beast, and in another version, she was trapped inside her castle by the monster, which had taken up residence in its only well. There are dozens of twists on the story, but they all agree that the girl was beautiful, the dragon ugly, and St. George the hero of the day. The dragon's skeleton was never reconstructed in London's Natural History Museum, but you don't have to travel far in England to find some representation of the hero on the back of his horse with a broadsword over his head, ready to strike the mortal blow to the writhing creature under him.

And just as surely as a dragon will always be part of the history of England, a lion and a unicorn will always grace its royal coat of arms. The lion is real enough. Its form has been a symbol of majesty since the ancient Assyrian kings compared themselves to the big cats. The earliest Egyptians decided that the king of beasts controlled the annual floods on the Nile to make their farms more

◆ *THE CHINESE DRAGON* (LEFT) *IS REGARDED AS A SYMBOL OF HEAVENLY GOODNESS. IN CONTRAST TO THE CHINESE, WESTERN CULTURES PRESENTED DRAGONS AS FORCES OF EVIL* (BELOW). ◆

productive. And because of that belief, the Greeks and Romans adorned fountains and springs with representations of them. The early Christians were fascinated by them, too, but they couldn't seem to make up their minds whether lions represented their redeemer or the devil himself. By the twelfth century, heraldry developed for the crusaders established lions as the ultimate symbol of strength and courage, and that's how the king of beasts found its way to England's coat of arms. The unicorn, on the other hand, is quite a different animal.

The unicorn seems to have been invented by our Stone Age ancestors, but it didn't find its way into the world's imagination until about 400 B.C., when a Greek historian returned home from a long sojourn among the Persians. When his countrymen tired of hearing about his adventures there, he began telling them tales he had heard about the wonders of India. Though he admitted it was all hearsay, everyone was fascinated by the creatures he described, including the manticora, a lionlike beast with the head of a man and a spiny tail it used to kill any animal, except an elephant. According to the legend, it also took great pleasure in chewing its victim into bite-size pieces with its three rows of razor-sharp teeth. What made the stories especially fascinating was that the manticora considered humans a special delicacy.

The same historian also introduced Europeans to the griffin, a feisty monster that was half lion and half eagle, but the most intriguing of all the animals he described was a type of wild donkey about the size of a horse with a horn on its forehead. Its body was white, its head dark red, and its eyes were the color of the sea. Its eighteen-inch horn was pure white at the base but turned jet black and then crimson before coming to a spearlike point. A beautiful animal, to be sure, but the unicorn was much more than that. It had

magical powers. Dust scraped from its horn could counteract the effects of any drug, and if the horn was used as a drinking vessel, it could make one immune to convulsions. Not only that, but that same liquid would also become an antidote to any poison. It made the horn a handy thing to have but, of course, they were extremely rare. The unicorn was said to be the fastest animal alive, making it nearly impossible to catch one. Aristotle believed it. So did Julius Caesar. Most important, so did St. Jerome, who became the first to give the creature the name *unicorn* when he translated the Hebrew Bible from Greek into Latin.

Unicorns were a perfect match for medieval imaginations. It was decided that the only way to catch one was to have a virgin sit quietly in the shade of a tree and sooner or later any unicorn in the neighborhood would have an irresistible impulse to lay its head in her lap. At that point, hunters would come out from hiding and easily capture the distracted creature. It wasn't as easy as it seemed, but during the first century, a fair number of what were purported to be unicorn horns turned up in castles all over Europe. As late as the sixteenth century, England's Queen Elizabeth I had one and it was considered a priceless treasure in the royal collection for more than a century. It was quietly removed when a scientist proved it had grown from the skull of a narwhal, a small whale that lives in cold Arctic waters. His theory was that all of the so-called unicorn horns in Europe had been collected from narwhals by Vikings, who turned them into a profitable business.

But old ideas die hard. Most Europeans had never seen a narwhal and many chose not to believe they existed. None of them had ever seen a unicorn, either, but as recently as 1906 a British explorer stunned the world by bringing a pair of one-horned goats out of Tibet. They turned out to be a fraud, but until it was proven that the Tibetans had been tampering with nature, some zoologists were ready to concede that unicorns did, in fact, exist. And who knows? One may turn up one of these days. In the meantime, there are hundreds of curious creatures out there that are very real and very strange.

✦ ACCORDING TO SOME STORYTELLERS, ANYTHING WE CAN DO ANIMALS CAN DO JUST AS WELL. ✦

✦ THE GRIFFIN IS A CREATURE OF FIRE, AND ITS LIKENESS OFTEN EMBELLISHES CANDLESTICKS. ✦

♦ CHAPTER ONE ♦

MAMMALS, PRIMATES, AND MARSUPIALS

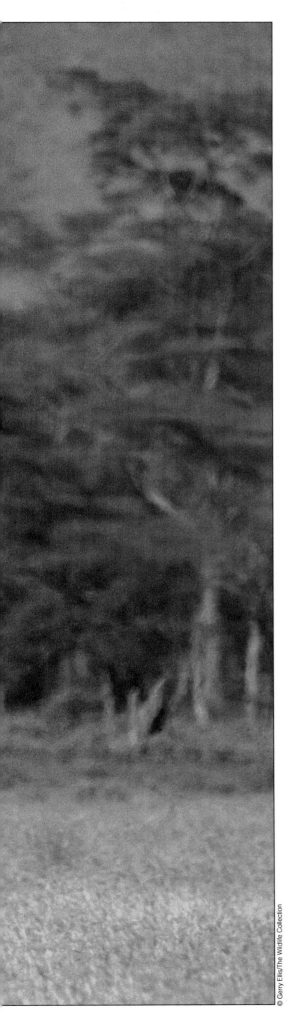

A Face Only
✦ A Mother ✦
Could Love

It has generally been concluded that the legend of the unicorn originated with the rhinoceros. But even without a legendary background, it ranks high among nature's curiosities because of its incredibly thick hide and its agility in spite of its awesome size, not to mention its appearance. Of the five different species of rhinos that live in Africa and Asia, two have a single horn. All rhinos are on the endangered species list because in many parts of the world, their horns are ground into a powder with the alleged magical power to cure almost anything that ails you. The powder can cost as much as fifty dollars an ounce.

✦ *THE BLACK RHINOCEROS CAN RUN AS FAST AS FORTY MILES AN HOUR ACROSS THE EAST AFRICAN PLAIN.* ✦

© Gerry Ellis/The Wildlife Collection

© Nancy Adams/Tom Stack & Associates

Though the African black rhinoceros, like its Indian cousin, weighs as much as two tons and can run forty miles an hour, hunters say it is easy to kill, probably because all rhinos are hopelessly nearsighted. They rely on their sense of smell to find their way around, but they are protected from danger by a small bird called an oxpecker. The bird is the rhino's constant companion, feeding on the ticks and flies the huge beast attracts. When something bigger than an insect comes into view, the bird responds with a chattering that serves as a warning. Sometimes the rhino won't do much more than raise its head and smell the air; it isn't easy to get four thousand pounds in motion. Usually the oxpecker's warning will send it into a run, but the rhino very often runs in the direction of the danger, rather than away from it.

Except for the birds riding on their backs, most rhinos are loners. They aren't hostile to each other, but if two of them are on the same path they'll usually make an elaborate detour to avoid meeting. Females will tolerate their calves for two or three years, but eventually they drive them away, and the parting is made so unpleasant that the youngster will usually go into an entirely different range.

✦ *THE RHINO'S THICK, ARMORLIKE HIDE MAKES IT AS STRONG AND INDESTRUCTIBLE AS A TANK.* ✦

© Gerry Ellis/The Wildlife Collection

If it can avoid poachers, a rhinoceros can live thirty or forty years. It reaches maturity at about the age of four and then seems to dedicate the rest of its life to doing as little as possible. They are as set in their ways as an old man and they seem to do exactly the same things at the same hour every day. Rhinos take a short walk at daybreak and then have a light breakfast of bark and leaves. When the

sun is completely above the horizon, they take a nap. They don't lie in the shade but seem to prefer sandy spots with full sun. In the late afternoon, they move to a mud hole, and in the evening they usually go for a swim; but not if getting to the water involves a long walk. A rhino drinks in moderation, usually not more than twice a week, getting most of the moisture it needs from the plants it eats.

But for all of its slow-moving laziness, surprising a rhinoceros can become a terrifying experience for a human or an animal. A rhino is able to go from a deep sleep to a dead run in just seconds, and even if it's only trying to get close enough to see who's there, being nose to nose with a face like that is not likely to be one of life's more pleasant experiences.

✦ *MOST RHINOS ARE LONERS, BUT THEY NEARLY ALWAYS TRAVEL WITH LITTLE BIRDS ON THEIR BACK.* ✦

MAMMALS, PRIMATES, AND MARSUPIALS

NOT THE
✦ AVERAGE ✦
TEDDY BEAR

All animals have Latin names, but unless you're a zoologist or a Latin scholar, most of them don't seem to mean much. But there is one that stands out like the skull and crossbones on a bottle of poison: it is *Ursis horribilis*, better known as the grizzly bear. And, curiously, though they often may look huggable, they are the fiercest mammal on the face of the earth.

Ursis means bear, *horribilis*, means what it says, and even the word *grizzly* takes on a special meaning in the northern Rocky Mountains and Alaska, where this five hundred-pound creature roams the woods. Actually, *grizzly* refers to the grayish tips of its fur, which is one of the few ways to tell the differ-

ence between it and the Alaska brown bear. There is even some question as to whether there is any other difference between the two, except that the brown bear is bigger, sometimes twice as big. The argument is generally settled by saying that brown bears live along Alaska's southeastern coast to the end of the Aleutian Islands and range inland for about fifty miles. All the rest are classified as grizzlies.

In general, it's best not to get near enough to either a brown bear or a grizzly bear to find out which is which. They have sharp claws five inches long, kept filed by long hours of digging for roots, and they are strong enough to kill a moose with one blow. They are also strong enough to pick up its eight hundred-pound carcass and carry it off without dragging it on the ground. And though they prefer eating mice and squirrels, grizzlies will attack anything that moves, even man, and almost always wins the battle. Back

✦ GRIZZLY BEARS MAY LOOK FRIENDLY, BUT DON'T EVER TRY TO PET ONE…AND DON'T TURN YOUR BACK ON A GRIZZLY MOTHER AND HER CUB (RIGHT); THE CONSEQUENCES COULD BE FATAL. ✦

© Thomas Kitchin/Tom Stack & Associates

© Gary Milburn/Tom Stack & Associates

in pre–Gold Rush days in California, when they were common in the Sierra Nevada Mountains, gamblers often pitted grizzlies against bison, and seldom lost any bets against the bears.

But to all intents and purposes, grizzlies seem like peace-loving creatures. Usually the largest male in the group dominates it, but he doesn't start a lot of fights to prove his superiority. One battle usually does the trick, and the loser is never driven away, but is allowed to stay in the community as long as it's properly respectful of the boss. Even the fiercest leader will back down to females with cubs.

The hierarchy among grizzlies is flexible. The dominant male has the right to the best fishing holes and gets first choice at other food as well. But he makes sure no one goes hungry. Grizzlies come together most frequently in July, when the salmon begin to spawn. The fish swim with the tide, which means that fishing is good for two short peri-

◆ "WHAT'S FOR DINNER?" FISH, MAINLY SALMON, IS USUALLY ON THE MENU, AND GRIZZLIES NEVER TIRE OF IT. ◆

ods each day. Instinctively the bears know when those periods are, almost as though they keep tide tables in their dens. The first salmon to be caught are eaten whole, and as the grizzly's hunger is satisfied, it gets more selective, feeding for a while on salmon steak and eventually concentrating on just the roe from the female fish.

In addition to seeming to be able to predict the tides, grizzlies are good weather forecasters, too. When September brings shorter

days, they leave their feeding grounds and begin digging the den where they'll hibernate for the winter. They always enter it during the first heavy snowfall when the snow will cover its tracks. No matter when the snow begins to fly, the grizzlies are ready for it. Even if the digging has been finished for weeks and they have gone back down to lower elevations for some last-minute feeding, they are always in their dens just as the first flakes start flying.

✦ *IF YOU'RE EVER CLOSE ENOUGH TO LOOK A GRIZZLY IN THE EYE, KEEP YOUR OWN EYE ON THOSE CLAWS.* ✦

POETRY
✦ IN ✦
MOTION

Hunters make sport of killing just about any creature that moves, and though they are often criticized, the one animal that earns them almost universal censure is the giraffe. Yet paintings in east African caves suggest it was one of the first creatures ever hunted because its long, tough hide was perfect for making bowstrings. The early white settlers in South Africa found it the best possible hide for making bullwhips. In spite of all their efforts, game hunters didn't do enough damage to endanger the species. Still, the giraffe is under the protection of tough game laws, since it doesn't seem sporting to kill one of these creatures that appears to be the gentlest in the animal kingdom.

The gentle giraffe isn't without defenses. Its massive head, with protruding bones that look like horns, has all the impact of a wreck-ing ball when it's swung at the end of that long neck. And a kick from its powerful hind legs can send a lion sprawling. Fortunately for lions and hyenas and the giraffe's other neighbors on the African plain, such demonstrations of strength are rare, though memorable enough to allow it to live in relative peace. Even males battling each other for dominance seem reluctant to resort to physical violence. Their fights are more like a ballet than a battle. Two bulls in such a contest will sidle up to each other and begin winding and unwinding their necks together very slowly. The process, not surprisingly called "necking," can last up to an hour until one or the other decides he's had enough. Sometimes, but not often, the neck wrestling degenerates into a swinging match in which each tries to butt the other and both move their necks in wide arcs to avoid being hit. If one is, chances are he'll be knocked unconscious by the sledgehammer-like blow.

Giraffes move in groups but don't seem to have any special attachment to each other. The makeup of a herd changes constantly and

✦ *THE GENTLE GIRAFFE HAS ALWAYS BEEN A FAVORITE SUBJECT FOR ILLUSTRATORS, BUT ITS LOOKS ARE EVEN MORE GRACEFUL IN PERSON.* ✦

© Gerry Ellis/The Wildlife Collection

even mothers with calves don't seem too concerned if the youngsters wander off. In fact, not long after the babies are born, they band together among other calves, sometimes with no adult nearby, while their mothers are off taking care of themselves. By the time they are eighteen months old they are completely on their own. The babies are six feet tall when they are born and reach their full height of about fifteen feet by the time they are five. But long before they reach full size, they are well established as loners, tolerant of their own kind, but always aloof from them.

Their individuality is further expressed by the markings on their hide, each as different from other giraffes as human fingerprints are different from one another.

Even when completely alone, giraffes are protected from danger by their keen eyesight. The fact that their eyes are so far above the ground would be an advantage in itself, but a giraffe can spot a lion miles away. If it feels threatened it can be miles off in another direction before the predator picks up its scent because it can run as fast as thirty-five miles an hour.

MAMMALS, PRIMATES, AND MARSUPIALS

A Tiger ✦ With ✦ Spots

One of the wonders the Italian explorer Amerigo Vespucci described having seen after his explorations of South America in 1500 was a panther. Later Spanish explorers claimed that the animal wasn't actually a panther at all, but a tiger. Today, the animal in question is still known in Spanish America as "el tigre." All of these monikers are wrong, however. What they were describing was in fact a jaguar, the biggest wildcat found in the New World. It has characteristics that were once thought to be unique to other branches of cats and has evolved into what can be called the ultimate cat.

The jaguar has black spots on its head, neck, and legs, and large rosettes with dots in the center running along its shoulders and back. At the center of its back, the spots sometimes run together, almost forming a stripe, which in a vague way may suggest a tiger. In some parts of Brazil it is not uncommon to see dark brown and black jaguars, which may have caused them to be confused with panthers or leopards. But the jaguar is in a class by itself. It is much heavier and more powerful than a leopard and, though shorter, is more heavily chested and more powerful in the legs than a tiger. Its head is larger than a tiger's, too, and though its face is shorter, the jaguar's teeth are the best developed of any of the big cats.

At one time, jaguars ranged into North America and one was seen in Arizona as recently as the late 1940s. They were also found in all parts of South America as far west as the Andes and south to the Straits of Magellan. Today they are largely confined to Mexico and Central and South America as far south as central Bolivia. Most of them were driven toward extinction by hunters who realized from the days of the conquistadores that their beautiful pelts were as valuable as the gold they had traveled so far to find. Even today, with their number steadily dwindling, thousands of jaguar skins are finding their way to furriers' workrooms, generating enough income for poachers to make the risk of killing them seem worthwhile.

The jaguar is not a model of catlike grace. In fact, it seems rather clumsy. But when attacking, it runs faster than most other cats and, unlike other members of the cat family, including some that are smaller, it is a good tree climber and often takes to the trees in search of its next victim. For all its power, the jaguar usually preys upon small animals. Its favorite food is a two-foot-tall guinea pig-like rodent called a capybara or a wild pig called a peccary. No small creature is safe from a jaguar, whose greatest challenge seems to be cracking open an armadillo or turtle shell. South America is not big-game country and the jaguar, though well equipped to hunt larger animals, never finds an opportunity for bigger kills.

In many remote parts of South America it isn't uncommon for farmers to capture small jaguars as pets, even though there is plenty of documentation that a full-grown animal is capable of attacking and killing humans. There is no question that they can be as intimidating as a junkyard dog, but by the time they begin to mature, they usually have to be returned to the wild. Beautiful as they are, jaguars don't take kindly to being someone's pet.

✦ *THE JAGUAR COMBINES NEARLY ALL OF THE BEST QUALITIES OF EVERY MEMBER OF THE CAT FAMILY.* ✦

MAMMALS, PRIMATES, AND MARSUPIALS

✦ LAZYBONES ✦

One of the most remarkable things about a sloth is that it wears a permanent smile on its face. The more you watch one, the more you realize that it has a lot to smile about. You'd be smiling, too, if you got nineteen hours of sleep each day. That's a conservative estimate made by patient sloth watchers. The question is, how did they know when it was awake? Even during the five hours a day the sloth is active, its movements are, well, slothful.

But beyond its good-natured smile and its effortless life-style, the sloth would rank among the animal kingdom's oddities for several other reasons. It spends most of its life hanging upside down in trees and because of its lack of movement, the algae that coats the tree limbs also covers the sloth's fur, making it quite hard to tell the difference between sloth and tree. It never finds the time to build

✦ A SLOTH ISN'T VERY FOND OF MOVING, BUT IT DOESN'T NEED TO. IT SURVIVES ON JUST A FEW LEAVES A DAY. ✦

a nest and usually curls up on any nearby tree when it gets tired, which is often. Its windpipe and gullet are unusually long, and it has more vertebrae than a giraffe in its short neck, even though the average sloth is only two feet tall, which allows it to turn its head in a complete circle. While hanging by one leg it is able to twist its body a full 360

NATURE'S CURIOUS CREATURES

degrees. Sloths are also unusually strong and can stretch their bodies from one tree to another, supporting their full weight in a horizontal position with the muscles in their legs.

Naturally, they don't perform that feat very often, it's too much like work. But hunger can drive a creature to great effort, and if a leaf or a flower across the way looks tempt-ing, the sloth will rise to the occasion. Hunger doesn't come often, though. Because its metabolism rate is nearly nonexistent, a sloth considers itself well fed if it gets three or four leaves a day. If a great deal of effort is required for it to get food, it can go several days without eating any leaves at all. It will eat in any position it happens to be in when

◆ *USUALLY JUST HANGING AROUND IS A FULL DAY'S WORK FOR A SLOTH.* ◆

◆ SLOTHS ENJOY CLIMBING TREES—IF THERE HAPPENS TO BE A GOOD SLEEPING BRANCH UP THERE. ◆

food is near, even hanging upside down. But it prefers to sleep cradled in the branches of a tree, curled up into a ball of fur with its head tucked under an arm. If something under the tree disturbs it, the sloth's only movement will be to lazily sweep the general area with one of its arms and then go right back to sleep. A half hour or so later, it will make the sweeping movement a second time just in case the first swat missed and the intruder is still lurking there.

Sloths never drink, seeming to get all the moisture they need from the dew on the leaves they eat. But if they don't drink water, they don't mind playing in it once in a while. Their thick fur is full of air pockets, which make them buoyant, and their strong arms make them fast swimmers. In fact, the only time sloths ever move any faster than a crawl is when they are in the water, which isn't often. One South American who has been observing sloths for a lifetime has suggested that this is because when they are swimming they can't stop to take a nap and are in a hurry to get on dry land for a much-needed rest.

THE KING
✦ OF THE ✦
UNDERWORLD

Every year, suburban gardeners spend millions of dollars trying to get rid of moles. Almost no one has ever seen one dead or alive, and when the mole's little hills stop appearing on the front lawn, they are never sure if they've killed it or if the mole has simply decided to move on to greener pastures. A mole can dig forty-five feet of tunnel in an hour and in the mating season, it moves three times as far.

Gardeners might do well to save their money. These little mammals can do some damage to roots and bulbs, and the hills they create burrowing just under the surface are unsightly, but what they're doing down there is eating worms and grubs. Typically, they eat more than their own weight every single day. Just as important, they aerate the soil and provide space for the accumulation of underground water.

Moles are completely adapted to their underground environment. They don't have external ears, and though they are not completely blind, they can't distinguish objects, only light and dark. They experience very little of the former and because night and day are all the same to them, the rhythm of their lives doesn't take its cue from the sun as is the case with nearly all other mammals. They burrow and eat for three or four hours and then rest for an equal amount of time. Their lack of eyesight is compensated by sensitive hairs on their nose and front feet that allow them to feel their way around. Their internal ears are tuned to vibrations in the soil around them, which not only keeps them alert to danger, but helps them hear other creatures that may turn out to be a tasty snack.

There are several varieties of moles that live in different parts of the world, but among them only some North American species ever come out of the ground. Some of these even climb into bushes. Even the most adventuresome moles prefer the safety of their tunnels. Even there, they are not completely safe. Exterminators are always on the lookout for signs of them, and until recently trappers also searched for their burrows. A mole's fur feels like velvet and it is unusually thick, making it valuable to furriers who used it for trimming or for making entire coats and jackets. Since its average size is just about five inches, it takes quite a few moles to meet even a small demand. At the height of the fur's popularity, some six million moles a year were killed in the name of fashion.

✦ *MOLES DON'T COME OUT OF THE GROUND VERY OFTEN, AND WHEN THEY DO, THEIR EYES ARE TOO WEAK TO SEE ANYTHING.* ✦

MAMMALS, PRIMATES, AND MARSUPIALS

THE ✦ CHINESE ✦ CONNECTION

One of the things we humans believe separates us from other animals is that we have thumbs and they don't. However, there is one other animal that does have a thumb. The giant panda of China's mountain provinces have, in addition to five normal digits on each paw, a sixth appendage that it uses in the same way we use our thumbs. It lives exclusively on bamboo shoots, and once it has pulled away a tempting branch, it holds it in its paws to strip away the leaves and eat the fibers. The thumb makes the job easy.

The panda's thumb isn't quite like ours. It is really just an extension of its wrist bone with a muscle that allows it to be moved. Using the bone like a thumb seems to be the panda's own invention. Its cousins, the bears, have similar bones and muscles but their preference for eating meat and fish have made such a thing useless. The panda, in fact, has only refined the sixth digit on its front paws. The ones on its feet are nearly nonexistent.

Chinese writers described giant pandas as far back as four thousand years ago, but the Western world never dreamed they existed until 1869, when the French Jesuit naturalist, Père Armand David, wrote about them. His writings were almost completely ignored. Another fifty years went by before another missionary, J. H. Edgar, climbed a mountain in China and was surprised to find a panda sleeping under a tree.

And what a pleasant surprise it was. Edgar couldn't resist the creature. Père David's description was based on pelts he had seen, but a live panda lying on its back chewing a branch held in its paws is one of nature's most irresistible sights. The black patches over the eyes and black ears above a white face, along with its black legs and shoulders and a soft white belly that looks like a bear cub's, add up to a cuddly creature, even though a full-grown panda is six feet long and weighs three hundred pounds.

The panda has a life expectancy of about fifteen years. Females give birth to one single-pound cub at a time, and can't expect to produce more offspring for another two years. They have few natural enemies, except wild dogs and leopards. Though they are vegetarians, they have the powerful jaws and sharp teeth of carnivores.

There is no accurate count of the number of pandas in China's high mountain bamboo groves, but the number is not more than a few hundred. They are protected by stringent laws that apparently have been successful in keeping them off the endangered species list.

✦ *NOT MUCH MORE THAN A CENTURY AGO PANDAS, ALONG WITH CHINESE DRAGONS, WERE THOUGHT TO BE IMAGINARY CREATURES.* ✦

BACK ✦ FROM ✦ EXTINCTION

Of all the species of mammals on earth, only one, Père David's deer, has never been seen in the wild by modern man. In fact, it is a species that became extinct as far back as two thousand years ago. Yet there are specimens in zoos all over the world today.

In 1865, the French missionary and explorer Armand David succeeded in gaining access to the private hunting park of the Chinese emperor near Beijing. During his stay, he became the first outsider to see this little four-foot-tall creature with a long tail that no one in the Western world even dreamed existed. Naturally, he wanted a specimen, but it took months of negotiations before a gamekeeper agreed to break the rules and smuggle out the hides and bones of a pair of them, which Père David secretly shipped home to Paris.

Zoologists were fascinated by the creature the Chinese had named "not like four," which they explained as "like, yet unlike a horse; like, yet unlike an ox; like, yet unlike a deer; and like, yet unlike a goat." It took years of diplomacy before the emperor agreed to allow a live pair to be shipped from his hunting ground to the zoo in London. Both animals died on the way. Eventually other pairs were shipped from China, which turned out to be a blessing for the species, because in 1894 a flood broke through the forty-five-mile-long walls of the imperial hunting ground and most of the deer escaped, all of them providing food for the starving peasants outside the walls. The few that were left were destroyed during the Boxer Rebellion six years later.

Hearing of the disaster, England's Duke of Bedford assembled about eighteen of the animals from European zoos and turned them loose on his estate, where it was felt they were more likely to reproduce than in the environment of a zoo. They thrived there, but during World War I, after seventeen years of breeding, a feed shortage reduced the herd to less than fifty. At that point, there were none left in China nor in any of the zoos of Europe. Since then, the population has increased again to a few hundred, and they have been redistributed among zoos in several countries, including China, where the saga began.

In addition to its unusually long tail and un-deerlike wide hooves, this deer's antlers face backward instead of forward, making them useless as a means of defense. But in its life in captivity, Père David's deer finds its antlers handy for scratching its back. During rutting periods, when the deer become sexually excited, the stag usually attracts attention to itself by covering its antlers with dried grass as if to impress the does with its ability to provide them with food.

In the summer, the deer is bright red with a black stripe along its back. In winter, when it wears an undercoat very much like wool, its color changes to dark gray.

✦ *PÈRE DAVID'S DEER HAS UNUSUAL BACKWARD-FACING ANTLERS, WHICH ARE COMPLETELY USELESS FOR DEFENDING ITSELF.* ✦

MAMMALS, PRIMATES, AND MARSUPIALS

In a
✦ Class by ✦
Itself

In the late eighteenth century, settlers moving into eastern Australia discovered a creature that had a bill and webbed feet like a duck and a furry body and tail like a beaver. Naturally, they had to tell the folks back home in England about this curiosity, and scientists there gave it the name platypus, meaning flatfooted, as if its feet were its most unusual characteristic.

In spite of eyewitness reports, most scientists flatly refused to believe that such an animal actually existed. Finally, in 1802, when a specimen that reached England was dissected, they had to admit the platypus wasn't a figment of Australian imaginations. But the experiment only proved to compound the mystery. The female's internal organs were quite different from any other quadruped,

and after a great deal of discussion, a French naturalist theorized that the platypus must be an egg layer. But others who had studied them pointed out that the creature had a four-chambered heart and a diaphragm like a mammal, which, as everyone knew, doesn't hatch its young from eggs. Still other scientists pointed out that it couldn't be a mammal because it didn't have mammary glands. It took nearly forty years of research and discussion before a German scientist discovered that the female secretes milk through her pores and her babies lick it from her fur. After bouncing through a half dozen different classifications, the platypus was finally accepted and welcomed into the family of mammals.

Scientists were still faced with that vexing question about the eggs. Finally, in 1884, a zoologist dissected another female and found a large egg encased in a leathery membrane very much like the reproductive system of a lizard. Rather than driving the creature from the ranks of the mammalians, they concluded

✦ *IF IT LOOKS LIKE A DUCK, THEN IT MUST BE A DUCK. IN THIS CASE, HOWEVER, IT ISN'T—IT'S A PLATYPUS.* ✦

that the platypus represented an early stage in the evolution of mammals from reptiles and birds.

The evolution took place more than 140 million years ago, so it is probably reasonable to assume that the platypus has been swimming in freshwater lakes and streams at least as long, even though it eluded human contact until just about two hundred years ago. It is still fairly successful, appearing occasionally at dusk but most often staying well hidden.

An accomplished swimmer, it uses its front webbed feet to move quickly in search of food. Its rubbery duckbill is perfect for straining insects and mollusks and other little creatures from the water. When swimming, it always closes its eyes and its ears to keep the water out. Its front feet are so extensively webbed that on land it needs to walk on its knuckles to keep its claws from puncturing them. Its hind feet have formidable spurs that are poisonous to its enemies.

✦ THE PLATYPUS HAS A BILL AND FEET LIKE A DUCK, BUT ITS TAIL IS JUST LIKE A BEAVER'S. ✦

A Taste
✦ For ✦
Canned Food

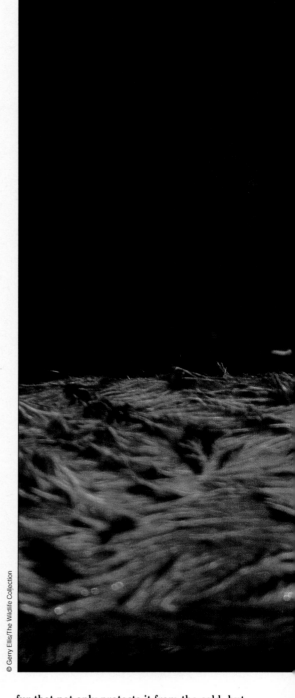

It's common knowledge that it is criminal to litter the landscape, but thoughtless people do it all the time, and tossing beer and soft-drink cans over the sides of boats is almost routine behavior. Strangely, in the waters off of America's Pacific Northwest, small octopuses turn the empty cans into homes. They are relatively safe in there and they are able to come and go through the little opening on the top. They are safe, that is, from every predator except the sea otter, who enjoys making a meal of these octupuses and has no trouble at all tearing the tops from the cans with its teeth.

Extracting sea creatures from their protective homes is rarely a problem for the sea otter, one of the few animals with the ability to use tools. It has a special fondness for shellfish, and when it dives to the bottom to collect them, it usually picks up a large, flat rock to make opening their shells easier. Coming to the surface, the otter floats on its back and uses its front paws to pound the shell on the rock until it cracks. It sometimes takes a lot of pounding to crack it, but the otter always wins. When the time comes to dive for more food, the otter puts the rock in its pocket—a long, loose fold of skin along its chest, which is used for storing such treasures as well as the shellfish it collects along the bottom.

Along with a pocket in its coat, the sea otter also wears a scarf—a furry fold across its shoulders—and mittens. The five toes on each of its forefeet are protected by a pad of fur that not only protects it from the cold, but also seems to keep it from accidentally breaking its toes when it is pounding hard shells on a rock.

A feeding sea otter is fascinating to watch. It floats lazily on the surface, propelling itself backward with its flipperlike hind feet. It usually has its eyes closed, though it looks over its shoulder occasionally to see where it is going. Unless it is busy cracking shells, it keeps its forefeet folded across its chest. If it is cracking shellfish, it gets a good grip on its

✦ *SEA OTTERS LOVE PLAYING IN THE WATER, BUT NOT UNLESS IT IS ICY COLD.* ✦

© Gerry Ellis/The Wildlife Collection

© Gerry Ellis/The Wildlife Collection

◆ *SWIMMING BACKWARDS IS ROUTINE FOR*

A SEA OTTER, USUALLY AFTER DIVING TO

THE BOTTOM FOR A SNACK. ◆

✦ *SOMETIMES AFTER A TRIP TO THE OCEAN FLOOR, A SEA OTTER COMES BACK DRAPED IN KELP.* ✦

rock and rolls over every few minutes to let the empty shells fall into the water. But no matter what it is doing, it stops quite often to preen its fur.

The sea otter's fur is unusually dense and the hairs are narrower at both ends than in the center, which allows air to be trapped between them to keep the mammal warm without a thick layer of fat underneath. But if dirt gets trapped there, the otter will freeze to death, which is one reason why it is especially vulnerable to oil spills. Because it is one

of the warmest furs in nature and because it hangs in loose folds on the otter's body, making a pelt much larger than the creature itself, it was a prime target for eighteenth-century fur hunters who almost succeeded in driving the sea otter to extinction. But like the recycling effect of discarded cans, there was a positive effect. The hunters, who were the first to seriously explore it, made the world aware of the wonders of North America's Pacific coast, not the least of which is the sea otter itself.

THE ✦ SWIMMING ✦ COW

When Europeans began taking long sea voyages, they were frequently impressed by a creature they saw swimming in the waters near India. It may have been the way the female nursed her young or possibly the animal's blunt nose and large but humanlike lips that made them think of mermaids. By the time they got home, their recollections were of beautiful nymphs and scientists were impressed enough to name the group *Sirena,* for the Sirens of Greek mythology.

When Christopher Columbus arrived in the Caribbean at the end of the fifteenth century, he was more scientific in studying them.

"They are not so beautiful as they are painted," he wrote. He was right. The scientists rolled with the punch and named it manatee, from a Latin root meaning "with hands." But they weren't quite right even then. Manatees don't have hind legs and their forelegs have evolved into flippers that don't even begin to resemble hands. But old legends are hard to put down and even the most scholarly scientists couldn't get used to the idea that manatees don't have human characteristics beyond the fact that they are mammals. Some of the explorers who followed Columbus to the New World put it in the right category by calling the creature *vaca marina,* "sea cow." What we know now is that the manatee was descended from a cowlike land animal more closely related to the elephant than it is to the cow that moved into the sea millions of years ago.

✦ *DIFFICULT AS IT MAY BE TO BELIEVE, MARINERS ONCE THOUGHT THAT MANATEES WERE MERMAIDS.* ✦

There was also some confusion between the animal Columbus observed, which was actually a manatee, and the one earlier explorers fell in love with, which was in fact a dugong, a very close relative. Both mammals have the same ancestors and both have been driven to near extinction because their meat is considered especially tasty, their oil unusually rich, and their hides a source of high-quality leather.

The manatee species in the Caribbean and West Africa, as well as the one that lives in the Amazon and Orinoco river systems of South America, are different from dugongs because they frequent fresh water and don't mind cavorting in brackish bays. Their cousins in the South Pacific, which sport tusks and have fishlike tails, prefer salt water.

All types of manatees are protected by conservation laws, but they have a fatal flaw in their extraordinary degree of friendliness and curiosity—frequently making them victims of the sharp propellers of passing boats.

They also seem to be prone to pneumonia, and when the water temperature drops below sixty-five degrees Fahrenheit, they usually get sick and die. They've found a way to beat the problem in Florida by gathering in large groups around power stations that pump warm water into rivers and bays. If the plants shut down, it can be a disaster. But while everything is working, industry, which is usually a prime suspect in the destruction of a species, may prove to be the biggest single factor in keeping manatees from vanishing from the face of the earth.

◆ MANATEES WERE SAFE IN THEIR UNDERWATER HOME FOR CENTURIES, BUT BOAT PROPELLERS HAVE BECOME A FORMIDABLE ENEMY. ◆

MAMMALS, PRIMATES, AND MARSUPIALS

THE
✦ EARTH ✦
PIG

If the creatures leaving Noah's Ark had come out in alphabetical order, the aardvarks would have led the parade. But such an honor wouldn't have pleased the aardvark. It goes out of its way to avoid contact with any other creature and has been seen so rarely by humans that as recently as the 1930s a hunter in southern Africa, who thought he had seen everything, recorded in his diary, "I received a dreadful shock. The beast was like nothing I had ever seen or imagined. It had a huge square head and the snout of a pig; its eyes, two black spots, were fixed on me with an observant stare. Large ears, the size of plates, stood up from its head, and they were transparent. The creature's body was covered with coarse brown hair; its tail was the size of a tree trunk." He was convinced he had seen the legendary proteus, a terrible bearlike animal described by Homer in the ninth century B.C. Actually, it was only an aardvark, a quite harmless 150-pound animal that was given its odd name, which means "earth pig," by early Dutch settlers in South Africa.

✦ *THE AARDVARK IS EVERY BIT AS HARMLESS AS IT LOOKS, BUT WHEN IT IS CORNERED, ITS SHARP CLAWS ARE FORMIDABLE WEAPONS.* ✦

Its body might be called bearlike, but the aardvark has a nose like a pig, ears like a rabbit, and a tail like a kangaroo. Its short legs are powerful and its toes consist of sharp claws. It can be a fierce fighter when cornered, but the aardvark just wants to be left alone. It even shuns the company of other aardvarks. It has a taste for ants and termites and occasionally feeds on fruit, but its claws are meant for burrowing and the aardvark is a master at it.

They spend the daylight hours deep inside their burrows, which often have as many as thirty openings and a network of underground tunnels that lead to a large gallery.

Their sharp claws make digging speedy and easy, and their long, thick tails make it simple for them to push aside the earth they dig. They begin digging when they are six months old. Never content with the homes they create, they dig a new one every couple of weeks. The tunnels and galleries they abandon become home to all kinds of creatures from snakes to squirrels to warthogs. During its nocturnal ramblings, an aardvark can cover as much as twenty miles before the sun comes up. In the process, they seek out termite mounds to dig up and get at the insects inside, which they catch with their long tongues coated with sticky saliva like flypaper. They almost never cover the same route two nights in a row, which explains why they are so rarely seen and why they are constantly changing their base of operation.

The hunter who thought the aardvark was staring menacingly at him had no way of knowing that the animal was having trouble seeing him at all. Like most burrowing creatures, its eyes are nearly useless. Its long ears make its sense of hearing especially acute, and its nose is sensitive enough to seek out a moving column of termites hundreds of yards away.

✦ AARDVARKS DON'T OFTEN COME OUT INTO THE DAYLIGHT, BUT THEY MOVE GREAT DISTANCES AT NIGHT. ✦

MAMMALS, PRIMATES, AND MARSUPIALS

A KNIGHT
✦ IN SHINING ✦
ARMOR

Deep in the heart of Texas, they say that the only way to make a decent pot of chili is to first get yourself an armadillo. But that's easier said than done. They're hard to find, for one thing. They are at home in open desert country, the hotter and drier the better, and they are forever digging burrows so that one is always handy where the little armored mammal can wedge itself in and give off an offensive smell that deters all but the most determined hunter. If there is no burrow nearby, the armadillo finds shelter in thick underbrush; even the spiniest cactus is no barrier, except to the hunter who drove it there. Better still, it can dig a new burrow in a matter of seconds, even in the middle of a paved road.

These cousins of the sloths are originally natives of South America, but eventually roamed into Central America and Mexico, and as recently as a few hundred years ago wandered across the Rio Grande into Texas. They are still exploring, but because they are not happy unless it is beastly hot, they aren't often found in the United States except in southern Texas. There are nearly two dozen different species, but the one that has become Americanized is the nine-banded variety, named for the number of flexible bands that connect its rigid armor plate. It is about three feet long and weighs fifteen pounds. Many of his cousins are much larger, but except for size, the family resemblances are striking, not to mention the most unusual in the animal kingdom.

They are the only mammals with armor-covered bodies and among the few that have no use for teeth, even though, unlike their relatives the anteaters, armadillos do have teeth. The giant armadillo of Brazil has more teeth than any other mammal, but they've evolved into stumps; the front teeth have disappeared because that same evolution has given them a long, sticky tongue for catching termites and ants.

Their armor is made up of small bones fused together and embedded in the skin. There is a separate helmet over the armadil-

◆ *THE BANDS ON AN ARMADILLO'S BACK ARE FLEXIBLE, ALLOWING IT TO MOVE IN SPITE OF ITS RIGID ARMOR.* ◆

lo's long, tapering head and the body armor hangs down over the sides like the chain mail draped over a knight's charger. The shell is solid in front and back and banded in the center to allow for flexibility. The armadillo's feet are also covered with hardened bone, but its neck and underside are soft and fleshy and vulnerable. To overcome that handicap, in times of danger the armadillo tucks its head between its front legs and rolls itself into a ball with only the tail sticking out.

But it has a better defense. The middle claw on the forefoot of the giant armadillo is the biggest and sharpest of any known animal and it uses it to dig through almost anything to create an instant burrow. Once a hole has been started, the creature props itself on its tail and uses all four feet for rapid digging.

The smaller armadillos of the American desert usually prefer to dash into the nearest thicket, where its armor allows it to get into places pursuers don't dare go. Before it runs from danger it has a self-defeating habit of jumping up into the air before dashing off, losing precious time and often getting caught for its indecision.

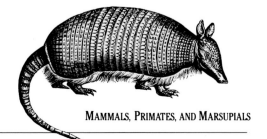

MAMMALS, PRIMATES, AND MARSUPIALS

THE
✦ MADDING ✦
CROWD

One of the great myths of the animal world is that in certain years in the north, millions of lemmings emerge from their burrows and rush headlong toward the sea, bent on mass suicide. It does happen, but what the lemming seems to have in mind is survival, not sudden death.

In late spring after a long winter underground, these little mouselike creatures come out from under the snow to mate. Spring and summer are short on the frozen tundra, but there is time enough for them to produce as many as five litters before winter sets in again. Normally, foxes and ermine manage to take care of any excess in the population, but in some years, known as "lemming years," their numbers grow beyond the availability of

food and the lemmings respond with mass migrations. In their hurry to find a new food supply, they don't stop to think about the hazards of crossing water and instead of going around it, they try to cross by jumping to drifting ice. In the process, most of them drown, and those that make it to an ice floe find themselves out in the open, where they are easy prey for ravens and owls.

The territory they have abandoned in the process will still be filled with lemmings for the rest of the summer, but in the following year and for several years to come none will be seen. It is one of the unsolved mysteries of the animal kingdom, and just as mysteriously they will eventually reappear.

Though they live in the Arctic, lemmings are essentially vegetarians like all other rodents. In the relatively warm months they thrive on willow leaves and the roots of grasses. In winter, they seem willing to eat anything at all, including small birds. During the summer, the lemming's fur is reddish

✦ *LEMMINGS MAY LOOK INSIGNIFICANT, BUT THEY ARE VERY IMPORTANT TO THE LIFE-CYCLES OF OTHER CREATURES IN THE FROZEN NORTH.* ✦

brown, but before the first snow begins to fly the fur thickens and turns white, providing the perfect camouflage. In all seasons, it spends most of its time in a deep burrow that protects it from storms and frost. When it does emerge, it is usually under cover of darkness. It wanders just about anywhere from the tops of mountains to the edge of the sea, avoiding only damp spots. The only requirement, it seems, is enough vegetation to eat. During the winter they do all of their hunting underground, searching for roots by digging long tunnels. They are well protected from the weather down there where hungry predators can't get at them, but they are vulnerable to changes in the weather. They are safe as long as the ground temperature is below freezing, but even a minor thaw sends moisture into their burrows and they are doomed to freeze to death.

Other creatures that share the lemming's environment suffer because of it. If the lemmings don't come out of the ground in the spring, foxes, which feed exclusively on them, are forced to watch their young starve to death; owls will neglect all but the strongest of their chicks, and ermines won't breed at all.

✦ *EVEN THOUGH THEY LIVE IN A LAND OF ETERNAL ICE AND SNOW, LEMMINGS ARE VEGETARIANS.* ✦

MAMMALS, PRIMATES, AND MARSUPIALS

A
✦ BAD ✦
REPUTATION

If you look up the word *shrew* in the dictionary, it is defined as a woman with a bad temper and a shrill voice. It is also a tiny little mammal that weighs only a few ounces and has been considered to be one of the nastiest creatures in nature since ancient times.

Mostly, it's a misunderstanding. Because the shrew is so little, it needs an unusually high metabolism to keep its body temperature stable, which makes it hyperactive and continually hungry. Shrews don't weigh much, to be sure, but they need to consume more than their own weight every day just to stay alive, and if it takes more than an hour or so to find the next meal, it will starve to death. The combination of its seemingly constant killing and its propensity for running at high speed to the tune of a shrill squeak have given it a bad reputation over the years. But the shrew is no more bloodthirsty than any other predators who need to kill to eat.

It is a fast runner, capable of speeds of up to two miles an hour. If that doesn't sound like much, consider the fact that ounce for ounce, the comparable speed in a human would be more than one hundred miles an hour. And as for the shrew's shriek, it is not the excitement of bloodlust, but a kind of sonar that allows it to find its prey and to find its way around. Like most burrowing animals, it has extremely poor eyesight.

But why is the dictionary sexist in its definition by noting that humans with shrewlike qualities are only women? Probably because in nature the female is much more aggressive than the male. It's only natural. She gives birth to a half dozen babies as frequently as every four months, and in addition to keeping herself from the brink of starvation she usually has other mouths to feed as well, which means she has to run faster and kill more often. It has been hinted for thousands of years that she usually kills her mate as if to thank him for the extra burden. But though cannibalism does exist in the world of the shrew, it seems to be a last resort in lean times and isn't restricted to either sex, although the female is always a more experienced hunter than the male and as a result is deadlier.

Shrews will eat just about anything they can catch. Insects and their larvae are first on the list, but a hungry shrew will attack a mouse or a frog larger than itself and usually win the battle. What they eat usually depends on where they live. There are about 265 different species that live in such varied environments as deserts and arctic tundra, as well as in forests and grasslands. There is no part of the United States that doesn't have a population of one kind or another, and there are millions of them right this moment devouring their own weight, and then some, in insects most of us consider harmful. But as hard as they work, they can't seem to live down their bad reputation.

✦ *EVEN SHAKESPEARE GAVE SHREWS A BAD NAME, BUT IT IS MOSTLY JUST A MISUNDERSTANDING.* ✦

NATURE'S CURIOUS CREATURES

PLAIN AS ✦ THE NOSE ON ✦ ITS FACE

The natives of Borneo called this creature "white man," but when white men finally reached the South Pacific island for the first time, the natives transferred their name for the proboscis monkey to these people.

The whites didn't know whether to be pleased or offended. Many species of monkeys resemble humans, but none except the proboscis has a protruding nose. Even more unusual is that youngsters and females of this species of leaf monkey have rather attractive noses. However, as an adult male matures, his nose never stops growing. And by the time he reaches full size, his nose is more of a nuisance than an advantage. It gets in the way when he tries to eat and he often has to resort to using one hand for climbing because he needs the other free to push aside branches so they don't hit him in the nose.

Never having actually seen a white man, the early Borneans didn't come up with their name for the monkey because of its nose. Its body is a reddish brown and its head is darker, but its face is pinkish white, and

✦ *PROBOSCIS MONKEYS RESEMBLE A LOT OF OTHER SIMIAN SPECIES, EXCEPT FOR THEIR UNUSUAL NOSE.* ✦

MAMMALS, PRIMATES, AND MARSUPIALS

when the monkey gets excited or overheated, the pink turns red. In these moments, a full-grown male looks very much like a caricature of an old man who drinks too much.

No one knows for sure why the proboscis monkey developed such an outlandish nose. Most theories are that it is a sign of virility that males use to attract members of the opposite sex. However, just as many experts hold that it is a means of enhancing their voice—always described, of course, as "nasal"—which is the monkey's way of asserting its territory.

Proboscis monkeys live mainly in large groups, typically including several males, along the banks of rivers and lakes and in mangrove swamps. They usually seem incapa-ble of moving very quickly, but when threatened they are incredibly adept at leaping great distances. They are also good swim-mers, able to cross large bodies of water and even able to stay submerged for thirty sec-onds at a time. Though crocodiles are among their natural enemies, they often take long swims to beat the heat. In fact, they enjoy playing in the water so much that they fre-quently stay in it a little too long. Sometimes other monkeys will swim out to rescue them when they are exhausted by a long swim, but more often they will be rescued by local fish-ermen whose seemingly humanitarian ges-ture is really self-serving. In Borneo the natives have a special fondness for proboscis monkeys. Roasted.

◆ THE MALE PROBOSCIS MONKEY HAS ONE OF THE BIGGEST NOSES IN NATURE. IT IS OFTEN SO BIG IT GETS IN HIS WAY. ◆

AN
✦ UNFORGETTABLE ✦
FACE

Most animals have evolved so that their color blends with their environment, camouflaging them against predators. But the mandrill is an animal of another color. The bridge of its nose is scarlet and its cheeks are furrowed with bright blue stripes. Its moustache and short beard are either orange or whitish yellow, and the side of its head is the same color, often becoming blue behind a white patch around its ears. Its fur is long on the top of its head and neck, surrounding the colorful, dog-like face like a lion's mane. Except for the underside, which is white, the mandrill's fur is dark gray with tints of green, and its hindquarters are deep red and bright blue, with highlights of purple.

Like protective coloration, the garish colors of the mandrill seem to be a defense mechanism. When it is threatened, the mandrill's first reaction is to stand up and fight, and when it does, the colors intensify. Its arms are heavily muscled and its teeth exceptionally sharp. When it rises to challenge a predator, even a leopard has reason to stand back and wonder if a mandrill dinner is worth the risk of being torn limb from limb. It's a fearsome sight. Though it's only three feet tall, the mandrill looks as though it can easily take on its weight and then some.

Like its relatives, the baboons, the mandrill lives on the ground, but its home is in the forest. Scientists believe that their ancestors lived in trees, but as climate changes wiped out their forest homes, they adapted to life on the plains. As the forests returned, the man-

drills went back. By then they had learned how to defend themselves on the ground and never bothered to look for refuge in the trees.

The remaining population of mandrills live in the rain forests of West Africa, where they feed on plants and small animals. When endangered by larger animals, they don't take to the trees, except at night, choosing to stand and fight as if there were no trees nearby. They tend to live in family groups consisting of a large male with a dozen females and their offspring. They are never far apart from one another and keep in touch with their voices. When they make eye contact, they signal friendliness by raising their lips to show their teeth, which to any other creature would seem to be a threat, but it is what passes for a smile. The smile turns to what might be interpreted as a friendly laugh when they chatter their teeth and shake their heads. On the other hand, when they don't feel like smiling, they show displeasure by yawning and smacking their lips. If they happen to be pounding the ground at the same time, it is a good sign to move on, as any forest-wise leopard will tell you.

✦ *MANDRILLS WEAR COATS OF MANY COLORS. WHEN THEY ARE ANGRY, THE COLORS BRIGHTEN.* ✦

MAMMALS, PRIMATES, AND MARSUPIALS

It takes a broad stretch of the imagination, but if Clark Gable were represented as an animal, he would probably be played by a tarsier. This little primate that lives in the jungles of the East Indies is more closely related to lemurs than it is to monkeys, but has most of the qualities of both. And it has more humanlike qualities than do some of the great apes.

Like the dashing star of *Gone With The Wind,* the tarsier's face has a fine, thin moustache on its upper lip, and its ears are slightly large and upstanding, but nicely flattened against its head. Because it is a nocturnal animal, its brown eyes are a bit large for the proportions of its rounded head, but they are surrounded by silky lashes that any movie star would be proud of.

Tarsiers are also great natural acrobats. It isn't uncommon to watch one sitting still on a high branch and suddenly, faster than the eye can follow, to see it in exactly the same position on another branch several yards away. It can jump up, down, or from tree to tree almost effortlessly with a speed that is hard to measure.

Little is known about what tarsiers eat. Some observers say they have a taste for fruit and tender leaves, but most agree that they are essentially meat eaters with a special taste for grasshoppers and an occasional lizard. And everyone who has studied them is impressed by their habit of sitting up on their hindquarters and eating with their hands.

Tarsiers are hard animals to observe. They spend most of the day asleep in the darkest place they can find, and because they don't make nests, their resting place varies from day to day. When they do venture out into the daylight their vision is so poor that in order to see a grasshopper they must lift it up to about an inch away from their eyes. At night their pupils enlarge making it possible for the tarsier to spot its next meal several yards away.

Even though they occasionally fight with one another over food, tarsiers are not especially aggressive creatures. They stay together in couples, and the female is usually able to take food, even from the male's mouth without any fuss at all. They produce one offspring at a time and the young stay with their parents for the few months it takes them to develop their tree-climbing skills.

✦ *LONG POWERFUL LEGS AND GRASPING PAWS MAKE TARSIERS NATURAL ACROBATS. ITS BIG EYES ALLOW IT TO SEE QUITE WELL IN THE DARK.* ✦

NATURE'S CURIOUS CREATURES

The Man
✦ of ✦
the Woods

According to a Malaysian legend, a race of men once displeased the gods, who condemned them to live in the green rain forest dressed in bright red fur. The natives called these red, apelike creatures orangutan, their word for "man of the woods."

When Europeans first saw these creatures in Borneo in the seventeenth century, they thought they had found proof that the mythical satyrs, long sought but never found, actually existed. One of them wrote that they had every quality of a human except speech, but noted that the natives had told him orangutans could talk but just didn't want to because they thought people would give them work to do.

In the nineteenth century, Edgar Allan Poe gave orangutans a bad name by making one the villain in his tale of "The Murders in the Rue Morgue." Two women were brutally murdered by a beast "...of agility astounding, a strength superhuman, a ferocity brutal, a butchery without motive, a grotesquerie in horror absolutely alien from humanity." The detective in the case followed a trail that led to an orangutan, starting with strands of red hair clutched by one of the victims and the handprints on the throat of the other that could not have been made by anything human.

While mystery fans were breaking out in cold sweats, Charles Darwin the scientist gave them something new to think about with his theories on evolution. When Darwin presented these theories to the scientific

community, he also read from the observations of Alfred Russell Wallace, who, at the time, was living in Borneo to study the habits of orangutans, and who had concluded that they represented an important link in the development of man from apes.

It all took some of the curse off the orangutan's image, and people began flocking to zoos to observe these creatures considered the elusive missing link. Many also found the same kinship in the chimpanzees of Africa, and their natural acting ability made them even more popular among zoo goers. But the orangutans in captivity showed that they had more practical skills. One of the first of them displayed at the San Diego Zoo figured out in a matter of days how to use its trapeze as a

✦ *THE SUMATRAN ORANGUTAN* (OPPOSITE PAGE) *AND ITS COUSIN FROM BORNEO* (ABOVE) *ARE OFTEN CONSIDERED MAN'S CLOSEST RELATIVE AMONG THE APES.* ✦

MAMMALS, PRIMATES, AND MARSUPIALS

© Brian Parker/Tom Stack & Associates

lever to pry apart the bars of his cage. He may have gotten away with it, but he took the time to assemble his blankets and favorite toys outside the cage before making his break for freedom. He was placed in a heavier cage, but figured out how to open it, too, and when he was placed in a third that had held grizzly bears in check, he not only escaped from it, but broke into a food storage room for a midnight snack. Beyond their desire to escape, orangutans seem to have an insatiable curios-

ity and no matter what is put into their cages to amuse them will inevitably be torn apart to find out what makes it work.

It seems predictable that eventually the only orangutans left in the world will be in zoos. The green rain forest that the gods were said to have banished them to is disappearing and their natural range has been reduced to parts of Borneo and western Sumatra. As the trees diminish, so do the numbers of orangutans in the wild state.

...And a Baby Named Joey

About 250 different species of marsupials carry their babies in a pouch, the most popular and well known being the kangaroo. The average adult male weighs about ninety pounds and when he balances himself on his tail and toes, he is six feet tall. At birth, kangaroos are only about three-quarters of an inch long and weigh less than an ounce. They have no ears and no eyes and their hind legs and tail are just tiny bumps. But their front paws are developed enough to let them crawl through their mother's fur and into her pouch. The distance involved is only about six inches, but it takes the baby about five minutes to reach its destination because it is completely left on its own. It will be another six months before it pokes its head out for its first look at the world.

As far as the world is concerned, the newborn kangaroo already has a name. All young kangaroos, male and female, are called ''joey'' by the Australians who consider them a national institution. But people never get their first look at little joey until it is eight months old and its mother decides the time has come to bend forward far enough to make the youngster tumble out of her pouch and onto the ground.

◆ *EVEN WHEN A YOUNG KANGAROO IS TOO BIG FOR ITS MOTHER'S POUCH, WHEN DANGER THREATENS IT FINDS SECURITY THERE.* ◆

MAMMALS, PRIMATES, AND MARSUPIALS

By then joey's legs are well formed, its ears are straight, and its fur thick, looking exactly like an eighteen-inch version of the giant it will eventually become. During its first excursion outside of the pouch, joey doesn't know what to make of it all. It will take a week of such trips before it finds out that its hind legs and thick tail were meant for hopping. When it makes the discovery, it can't seem to get enough of hopping around, and its mother encourages it to hop anywhere it can. Except back into the pouch. When danger threatens, she bends down so that the baby can reach her pouch and begins making soft sucking sounds to get its attention. The baby then dives in head first and quickly turns around to get its head outside to see what all the fuss was about.

The mother keeps her baby in the pouch every night and won't let it out in the morning until the sun has dried the dew. When she grazes, so does the little joey, but from inside the pouch where it is in no danger of getting its feet wet. The routine continues until the baby is about ten months old and weighs close to fifteen pounds. At that point it is evicted from the pouch forever, but it will stay with its mother for another eight months until it is big enough to go off on its own.

By then, a female joey is nearly full grown, but a male will continue to develop for another two years. The adult doe is rarely more than four feet tall and weighs less than fifty pounds. They spend their lives grazing on any kind of grass that is available. Though all kangaroos are capable of leaping over high fences and can run as fast as thirty miles an hour, they prefer to laze around chewing the grass and preening their fur. When threatened, the females bound away to safety, but the males usually prefer to stand and fight. Their greatest enemy is the Australian wild dog known as the dingo, and though they can easily kill a kangaroo, many dingoes are more often surprised when they get a murderous kick from their intended victim. Though they keep on trying and take their toll on the kangaroo populations, the majority of kangaroos die of natural causes. Nature has endowed them with weak teeth, and by the time the average kangaroo is twenty years old, its teeth have either fallen out or been worn down from a lifetime of chewing, and without teeth it is doomed to die of starvation.

© Gerry Ellis/The Wildlife Collection

© Gerry Ellis/The Wildlife Collection

NATURE'S CURIOUS CREATURES

A
✦ CUDDLY ✦
CHARMER

The face of a koala makes a perfect teddy bear because the koala, which is more closely related to kangaroos than bears, looks more like Winnie the Pooh than any bear that ever lived. The most famous koala has become a television star complaining that its native Australia is being overrun with tourists who disturb its daily routine. Until very recently, the koala had more to fear from Australians than from visitors. It wasn't until the 1930s that the government placed them under special protection to prevent their extinction from hunters and fur trappers. By then the koala population, which had numbered in the millions and ranged over all of Australia, was reduced to just a few thousand limited in range to a narrow band along the east coast.

✦ *THE KOALA'S WORLD IS AMONG THE BRANCHES OF EUCALYPTUS TREES.* ✦

A century ago, it was considered great sport to shoot koalas. But it was a sport tinged with cruelty. When it is hit, the koala utters a cry similar to that of a human baby. But koalas make easy targets. They are usually found at the top of eucalyptus trees where they have stripped away the leaves that might otherwise conceal them. The "sport" came into the picture because if a koala is simply wounded, it will continue to cling to the tree limbs. Its feet have two thumblike digits that give it a wrenchlike grip even if the animal is weakened. Unless a sportsman gets off a clean shot the first time, the koala will stay where it is to die slowly. Until restrictions were put in place, the koala's grayish silver fur brought high prices, and at the height of its popularity, it was one of Australia's major exports, resulting in the loss of more than two million koalas a year.

In their protected state, koalas are captured only for resettlement in other places where their ancestors once thrived. But it is a tricky business because the koala is a finicky eater: it won't eat anything except eucalyptus leaves. But not just any eucalyptus leaf will do. There are more than 350 different varieties of the tree in Australia, but koalas completely ignore all but twenty of them. And they also ignore many of the leaves on trees they do find acceptable, never touching new growth at all. When they are moved to new locations, even though their favorite trees are growing there, it is usually necessary to also move leaves from their original homes to tide them over the several months it takes them to get used to the local fare. Because of that, koalas are almost nonexistent in zoos, except in places like California and Australia, where there is a local food supply. It wasn't until quite recently that zoologists discovered

◆ *No matter what impression they give, koalas love people-watching.* ◆

something that koalas have known for hundreds of years: the young leaves and shoots of the trees contain a chemical that is poisonous to them. At the same time they discovered that the trees the animals completely shunned contained elements that could also kill them.

The koala is a marsupial, which carries its young in a pouch. But unlike other marsupials, the Koala's pouch faces backward. Once the baby is big enough to come out of the

pouch, its mother carries it on her back until it is about a year old, eliminating the problem of having it fall out when she is climbing through the trees.

In spite of all the problems people have caused them, koalas love humans instinctively and once they have become attached to someone they cry when they are left alone. They especially enjoy being carried around and have an endless curiosity about the things people carry around with them.

Nature's Curious Creatures

WHAT'S
✦ IN A ✦
NAME?

Farmers all over the world consider wolves their greatest enemy and they have succeeded in driving them to extinction in many countries where they once thrived. Sheep farmers on the island of Tasmania off the southeast coast of Australia may be among them. They haven't quite eliminated the Tasmanian wolf, but they've come close, and the remaining specimens have been driven into the forest from the plains that are their traditional hunting grounds.

Actually, this creature isn't a wolf at all. Some people call it a tiger because of the stripes on its back and its ferocious nature. But it isn't a big cat, either. It is a marsupial that carries its young in a rear-facing pouch. It resembles a wolf, but its hindquarters are quite different and its tail is thick and much more like a kangaroo's than a wolf's. There is another major difference, too. The Tasmanian wolf, which is the largest carnivorous marsupial, has the ability to open its mouth a full 180 degrees, its jaw forming a straight line. When it does, it displays forty-six sharp teeth.

Such a fierce-looking beast is bound to be the subject of myths, and any Tasmanian rancher will tell you—in spite of the fact that except for its footprints, none has been seen in the wild in more than fifty years—that they are the bloodthirstiest creatures on earth. According to stories, they will kill a sheep or a kangaroo by slashing its throat and sucking its blood, but never touching the meat. In captivity, they have proven to be quite voracious meat eaters.

The marsupial wolves don't hunt in packs like true wolves, and it is said that a pack of wild dogs, quite fierce in their own right, will run in terror from a lone Tasmanian wolf. The so-called wolves move along at a trot, but when speed is required they will rear up on their hind legs and hop like their cousins, the kangaroos. They are patient hunters and good trackers and will follow a potential victim until it tires before moving in for the kill.

Before man arrived in Tasmania there were few wild creatures safe from the Tasmanian wolf. The six-foot-long predator will attack animals much larger than itself, and its sharp teeth and agile jaw make any contest rather short. When it developed a taste for livestock, ranchers began setting poisoned traps for them, and if saving their flocks wasn't incentive enough, the government paid a bounty for them. Today that same government is protecting the Tasmanian wolf, and the fine for killing one is twenty times larger than the bounty. It may be too late. Of all the endangered species, the Tasmanian wolf may be the most endangered of all.

✦ TASMANIAN WOLVES ARE SOMETIMES CALLED TIGERS, BUT THEY ARE NEITHER CATS NOR CANINES. ✦

✦ CHAPTER TWO ✦

ANIMALS OF
THE AIR, ANIMALS
OF THE WATER

A Bird
✦ You May ✦
Never See

Except at the North and South poles, there are rails in every part of the world. There are 132 different kinds of these birds, from those that look like little sparrows, but with duller markings, to others as big as ducks, whose feathers are bright green and purple. Many of them can't fly, others migrate. They all have one thing in common: they are incredibly shy. Most people who have grown up familiar with their calls have never actually seen one, and if the rails have anything to say about it, they never will.

All rails have compact bodies and are able to wander through dense vegetation that has the effect of a solid wall to other creatures. They prefer walking to flying, and when they're forced to take to the air, they go straight up like a helicopter and then struggle off with their head extended forward and their legs trailing beneath them. The varieties that migrate don't seem to share the navigational instincts of other birds and often fly into hillsides and buildings—partly because they insist on traveling in the dead of night.

There is hardly an island in the world, from Iceland to Tahiti, that doesn't have a population of rails. They live in marshlands and on forest floors, along alpine lakes, in thick prairie grass, and at the edges of deserts. They are at home at sea level as well as at 16,000 feet above it. In many places, especially tropical islands where they have no natural enemies, rails have forgotten how to fly, but considering the lack of aerial grace among those that do remember, flight isn't something they enjoy anyway.

Though they seem compelled to hide themselves away, they do flock together in fairly large groups. Males and females breed for life and both take turns incubating their eggs. Their nests are usually made of any vegetation that happens to be handy: in a marsh, it is usually reeds and grass; in a forest it is leaves and bark, and sometimes even in burrows under tree roots. It is a rare rail that leaves its nest during daylight hours, but they come out in full force at night, when their shrill voices make them unpopular with people trying to sleep.

While one rail species that lives in New Zealand—the weka—shares the instinctive shyness of its relatives, it is one of the most aggressive members of the family. It is flightless, about the size of a chicken, but it is very fast on its feet, able to run down a rat or a mouse without any effort at all. It seems to enjoy the chase and its reward, but it much prefers raiding the nests of other birds and stealing the eggs, a habit that often leads it to human homes, where it will take anything it can carry off. Without ever being seen.

✦ *RAILS COME IN ALL SIZES, USUALLY WITH OVERSIZE FEET. THE VIRGINIA RAIL (BELOW) IS THE SAME SIZE AS A ROBIN.* ✦

NATURE'S CURIOUS CREATURES

© Gary Bell/The Wildlife Collection

✦ *The banded land rail makes its*

home in the Pacific islands. ✦

THE WORLD'S
✦ FRIENDLIEST ✦
BIRD

Anyone who has ever worked on a crossword puzzle knows that *emu* is a three-letter word describing a flightless bird. But this native Australian deserves to be known for more than that. It is the second-largest bird in the world, after the African ostrich. It is five feet tall, but would be much taller if it stood up straight. Its backbone runs almost parallel to the ground, a posture defect acquired from long hours of grazing in grasslands.

Its grazing habits make *emu* a dirty word among sheepherders and cattlemen in eastern Australia, where the big birds compete with their livestock for the available grass. Unfortunately, the birds are losing the battle and face extinction because of it. To help prevent that from happening, a 500-mile-long fence has been built across the Australian plain to keep the emus and the other grazing animals apart. But to the birds, at least, the grass is always greener on the other side and they are constantly attacking the fence with their powerful legs, sometimes managing to break through. Game wardens who are responsible for chasing them back have their work cut out for them because emus can run

✦ *THANKS TO CROSSWORD PUZZLES, THE EMU IS THE WORLD'S BEST-KNOWN FLIGHTLESS BIRD.* ✦

© Gerry Ellis/The Wildlife Collection

© Gerry Ellis/The Wildlife Collection

as fast as forty miles an hour, resulting in many a wild ride as the wardens give chase in their Land Rovers.

Emus are incredibly curious birds and will usually run up to the game wardens as if to have a friendly chat. They seem to genuinely like people and often seek them out, which is one of the reasons why they are so close to extinction. It is also a personality trait that makes them model zoo animals. They seem to thrive in captivity, and it's often hard to tell who's enjoying themselves more, the emus or the people who come to the zoos to see them. Ironically, they are closely related to the cas-

sowaries of the Pacific islands near New Guinea, one of the few birds capable of killing a human.

In the wild, emus share many of the less hostile habits of their cousins. Among them is the male bird's determination to incubate the eggs the female has produced. The females never seem to get used to the idea and almost always have to be driven off, but once the male has made his point, he takes over the job of not only hatching the eggs, but brooding and raising the young birds as well. And there probably isn't a prouder parent in the animal kingdom.

ANIMALS OF THE AIR, ANIMALS OF THE WATER

The Surfer
✦ With a Deadly ✦
Sting

In some of Florida's Atlantic coast resorts, local newspapers regularly publish predictions of water temperature and tides. But what is unique about their reports is that they also provide warnings when fleets of Portuguese man-of-war are on the way. If the invasion is expected to be heavy, the beaches are closed.

The floating menace is not the ghost of a rapacious fifteenth-century sailing fleet, but a fascinatingly beautiful creature that sails the waters of the Gulf Stream, killing, or at least seriously injuring, any other creature they may happen to touch. Fortunately for swimmers, they usually stay far out at sea, but a few days of easterly winds can drive them onshore, and late each summer the watch for them extends all the way up the East Coast of the United States as far north as New England. And in years when their population swells and the winds are just right, they menace the coast of Great Britain as well.

There are millions of Portuguese man-of-war out there, and they have been a problem for sailors and beachcombers for hundreds of years. But in spite of this, very little is known about them. No one knows for sure what its poison is, though most experts agree it is a combination of three different toxins. One of them paralyzes the nervous system, the second affects breathing, and the third induces a comalike state that can result in death. Most people who have encountered a Portuguese man-of-war in the water or on a beach suffer little more than a painful welt, but some have been known to drown after the shock of the sting. Others who have waded into a colony of them haven't survived.

What is odd about the man-of-war is that it isn't a single creature at all, but a group of individuals that have attached themselves to each other, each different from the other, and none able to exist without the rest. At the top is a floating jellyfish-like animal filled with nitrogen and oxygen that keeps it above the water and acts like a sail. It doesn't seem able to deflate the sail, and is largely at the mercy of the wind, which is why it often comes ashore. Below it is a different animal with trailing tentacles that extend into the water as deep as fifty feet. It has a venomous sting.

Nothing that swims is safe from them. But everywhere the Portuguese man-of-war sails, it is followed by small fish that are never seen anywhere else. It lives by scavenging the man-of-war's leftovers, and it stays alive by carefully avoiding its tentacles because it has never developed an immunity to the poison. In fact, there doesn't seem to be any such thing. In human contacts, an encounter with a cobra might be less deadly than tangling with a man-of-war fleet. The best remedy medical science has been able to produce is bathing a sting with seawater and cleaning it with alcohol and baking soda; for multiple stings, not much, apparently, can be done.

Obviously, a creature like this has no natural enemies. None, that is, unless you consider the sea turtle. They seem to think man-of-war tentacles are a delicacy worth any risk. But they aren't immune to the poison, either, and though they aren't able to resist attacking a Portuguese man-of-war, they pay a price for the meal in the form of painful swelling and a loss of coordination that makes them appear to be drunk.

✦ *THE PORTUGUESE MAN-OF-WAR IS A BEAUTIFUL CREATURE, BUT ITS TENTACLES CAN EASILY KILL A HUMAN WHO GETS TOO CLOSE.* ✦

The Flower
✦ of the Animal ✦
World

If you're walking beside a tidepool and are overcome by an urge to bend down to smell the flowers, don't be too surprised if you get stung on the nose. What you may have thought were beautiful flowers are actually sea anemones, and their petals are really tentacles that have thousands of tiny darts embedded in them. When a small creature gets close, the anemone fires a fusillade of darts at it that inject a poison into the victim, making it easy for the tentacles to grab it and force it toward the anemone's mouth. Even fish larger than the anemone itself aren't safe.

The sea anemone is one of the simplest of creatures on earth. Its body consists of a muscled cylinder with a disk at one end that has a mouthlike opening at the center and several rows of colorful tentacles surrounding it. The disk at the other end allows the anemone to slide slowly across the surface of rocks and it also acts like a suction cup that holds the creature in place with such force that it can't be torn away without completely destroying it. A tube hanging down from its mouth into its stomach is lined with tiny hairlike filaments that are constantly waving in a downward motion to carry a continuous flow of oxygen-rich water to the anemone's stomach. Other similar filaments beat in the opposite direction to carry off the anemone's carbon dioxide and waste. When the tentacles have trapped a potential meal all of the filaments beat in a downward direction to create a kind of swallowing action.

© Chris Huss/The Wildlife Collection

While such swallowing and digestion are taking place, the anemone folds its tentacles, closes its mouth, and blends into the background of the tidepool. When it's hungry again, it blooms like a flower and it is only a matter of time before some curious creature becomes its next victim. The anemone has plenty of time. Many have been observed in

✦ *The Christmas anemone* (opposite page) *and the Crimson anemone* (above) *both live in the Pacific Northwest. Other varieties thrive all over the world.* ✦

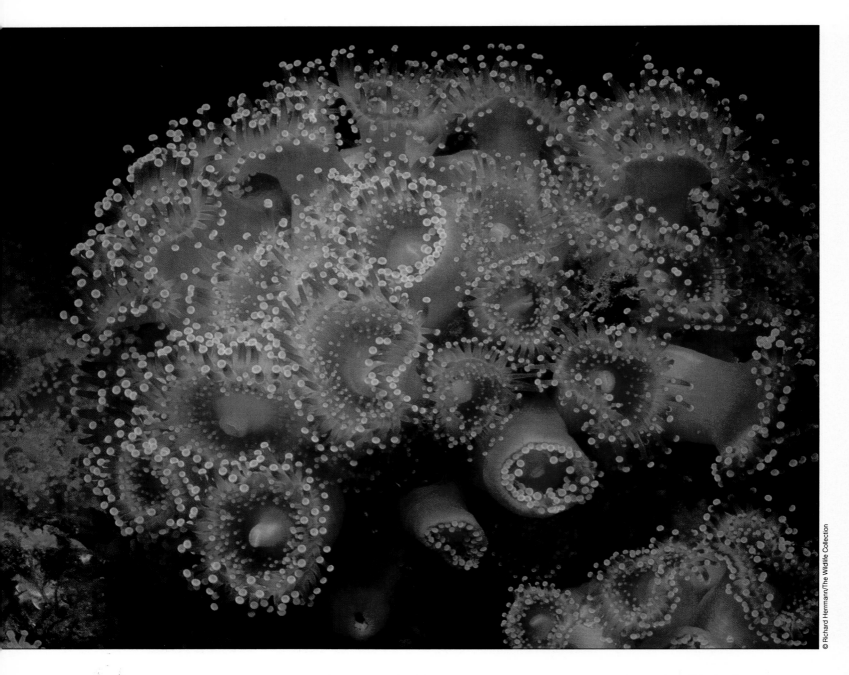

© Richard Herrmann/The Wildlife Collection

✦ *THE CLUB-LIPPED ANEMONE IS A NORTH AMERICAN VARIETY.* ✦

the same spot for fifty years or more and some have been known to survive in captivity for twice as long.

Anemones don't seem to have the problem of finding a mate. Some reproduce by simply dividing themselves in two. The offspring never move more than a few inches away, and as hundreds of repeated divisions take place, they form massive colonies. Others disperse the colonies by leaving behind slices of their lower disk as they move around. These disks eventually grow into full-size anemones. Still others lay eggs by ejecting them through their mouths in the hope that they will attach

themselves to a rock or a shellfish and become a new anemone.

Anemones thrive in shallow water, their large colonies looking like flower gardens as their colorful tentacles wave together above their translucent bodies. When the tide pulls the water away from them, they pull in their tentacles and contract their bodies into a flattened cone. Those that cling to the sides of rocks react to the withdrawal of the water by hanging limply in a mass that resembles the shape of an hourglass. When the tide flows back, the anemone takes it as a signal to turn into a flower again.

NATURE'S CURIOUS CREATURES

✦ STAR TREK ✦

There are more than two thousand different species of starfish, ranging in size from less than half an inch to almost three feet across. Most are shaped like stars with five arms or more, but some starfish form almost perfect circles. They come in a variety of colors ranging from bright red to yellow to pink and orange, but some are gray, green, or purple. Nearly all of them live on a diet of mollusks, but some have a taste for sea urchins and even other sea stars, and some swallow soft mud from the sea bottom to get at the nutrients buried deep within it.

But they all have a lot in common. Each of its arms is actually part of its body and at the end of each of them is a simple eye, usually marked by a red spot, that lets any arm become the head when it decides to move around. Also on the underside of each arm, which branch out from its mouth, the sea star has a groove containing a row of tube feet. But there are no feet on the top side, which causes a problem when it gets turned upside down. Sometimes it takes as long as an hour and a half to get things right again. The most common method is to bend all of the arms in the same direction, which causes its body to become rounded and off balance. When it falls over to one side, it laboriously curls the arms closest to the bottom and grabs hold with the tube feet. Once anchored, it tugs itself until another arm is anchored, and eventually all of them will be in place putting the starfish's mouth where it should be, facing downward.

Some varieties have discovered that it is easier and much faster to curl under two of its arms so the feet can attach themselves to

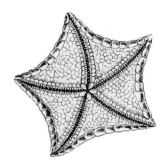

✦ *NOT EVERY SEA STAR HAS A BEAUTIFUL NAME. CONSIDER THE SPINY RED STAR.* ✦

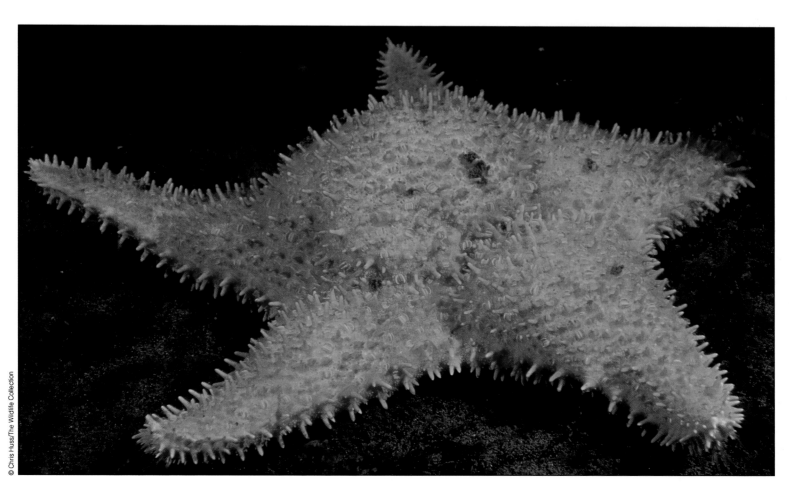

ANIMALS OF THE AIR, ANIMALS OF THE WATER

✦ *SEA STARS COME IN MORE THAN TWO*

THOUSAND VARIETIES, ALL OF THEM

BEAUTIFUL. ✦

NATURE'S CURIOUS CREATURES

the surface; then it simply walks under itself in a motion that resembles a somersault. But either way, its strong feet are the key to success. Each is a hollow tube with a strong, bulblike muscle. When the muscle is contracted water is forced into the cavity, then other muscles in the wall shorten it and the water is forced back into the bulb. The resulting action, repeated in a long row of the tube feet, moves the starfish along any surface, from soupy mud to solid rock. The tubes are slanted so that when they are filled with water they push against the surface and cause the animal to slide along in a shuffling gait. Most of the tiny feet have suction cup-like devices at their tips, but the ones closest to the ends of the arm contain sensors that can detect chemical changes in the water, announcing the presence of danger or of a meal.

✦ THERE MAY BE AS MANY STARS UNDER THE SEA AS THERE ARE IN THE SKY. ✦

✦ NATURE'S ✦ SUBMARINE

The principle that makes submarines able to dive to the bottom of the sea and come back to the surface again has existed in nature for more than 450 million years and still works very well for the chambered and paper nautilus of the waters off the Philippine Islands. In earlier forms, their spiral shells were as big as six feet around and weighed as much as three hundred pounds, but they rose and fell in the sea as though they were weightless.

Today the nautilus rarely gets larger than ten inches, but the buoyancy principle of its ancestors is still the same. The inside of its beautiful shell contains as many as thirty-five chambers behind the one that is actually occupied by the nautilus itself. Each of the chambers is connected to the others with a small tube that acts like a siphon to regulate the density of gas trapped inside to allow it to rise up to the surface of the water.

The nautilus shell is one of nature's most beautiful creations. It also fascinates mathematicians because its curvature follows a perfect logarithmic spiral, with each turn of the shell exactly three times the size of the one below it. As soon as the young are hatched from the egg, they set to work creating the shell, which begins as the size of a pea at first, but grows along with the creature. At each successive stage of development, the nautilus moves into a new chamber and seals off the one it has just left.

The chambered nautilus lives inside its shell, but the paper nautilus wraps itself around it, using the interior to protect its young. Two thousand years ago, Aristotle wrote that these creatures he called argonauts spread their arms before the wind and sailed from place to place. In fact, they are generally at home on the bottom of the sea, where they crawl in search of crustaceans, coming to the surface to breed.

The nautilus is a form of octopus, but instead of laying eggs in caves, the female of this species takes hers with her wherever she goes. While her young are still inside her shell, she does, indeed, use two of her arms

✦ *THE CHAMBERED NAUTILUS IS AN UNUSUAL MEMBER OF THE OCTOPUS FAMILY.* ✦

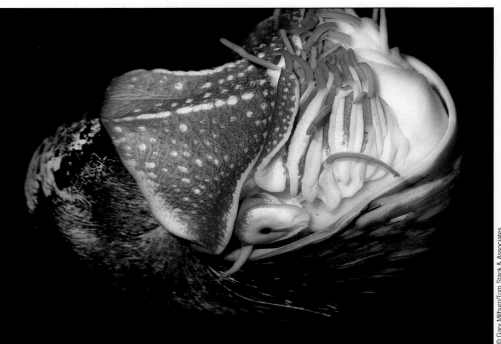

♦ *THE NAUTILUS SHELL IS OFTEN CONSIDERED TO BE ONE OF NATURE'S MOST PERFECT CREATIONS.* ♦

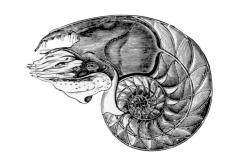

as sails, as Aristotle suggested, and uses the other four as oars to move about the surface in search of food. She is many times larger than her male counterpart and the diminutive mate usually swims a wide berth around her. Even while mating, a male doesn't risk tangling with those tentacles. One of its own eight arms is a sex organ that is detachable. It gets as close to her as safety will allow, sheds the arm, and moves away as fast as possible. It puts a big element of chance into a sexual encounter, to be sure. But to a nautilus, it is obviously better to have loved and lost an arm than to have been loved to death.

ANIMALS OF THE AIR, ANIMALS OF THE WATER

All
✦ IN THE ✦
Head

There are nine different kinds of hammer-head sharks, ranging from the bonnethead, which is about three feet long, to the giant great hammerhead, which can be as long as twenty feet. But they all have one thing in common, a head shaped like a hammer with an eye and a nostril at each end of the ''ham-mer'' and rows of sharp teeth between them. Even the little one has been known to bite divers, and its bigger cousin is one of the thirty-five different kinds of sharks classed as possible man-eaters. After the great white shark, it is the most dangerous shark in the waters off the United States.

The hammerhead's chief prey is stingrays, and they seem completely oblivious to the ray's stinging barbs, usually enough protec-tion against other predatory creatures. When a hammerhead swims, it swings its head from side to side, hunting for food both by smell and by sight. As one of its nostrils picks up a scent, the swinging motion soon picks up the same scent on the other side and the shark is able to coordinate them to pinpoint exactly where the next meal is. When the scent is weak, the hammerhead's eyes do the job for it in the same way.

Like many other sharks, the hammerhead also has a network of ducts in its head that make it sensitive to the slightest vibrations, making it simple to seek out prey buried in the mud at the bottom of the ocean. Mud is a favorite hiding place for the stingray, and it also has the ability to stay absolutely still and

✦ *THE HAMMERHEAD SHARK HUNTS BY SWINGING ITS HEAD FROM SIDE TO SIDE, ALLOWING IT TO PICK UP AND PINPOINT THE SCENTS OF ITS PREY.* ✦

therefore virtually invisible to predators. But the hammerhead has developed a way to find them. It also has sensors that can detect electrical fields. Every living creature gives off a weak electrical charge, and the stingray is no exception, so it can't hide from a hungry hammerhead no matter how deep it burrows or how still it lies. Other sharks find stingrays tempting, too, but the hammerhead is the world's champion stingray catcher.

Almost any creature in the sea is fair game for a hammerhead, and they have even been known to wolf down canned goods tossed overboard from passing ships. But of all the creatures sharing its warm water world, the hammerhead will usually swim a wide berth around a dolphin. It isn't that they are averse to dolphin meat, and the dolphin's teeth are no menace at all to a shark, whose sandpaper-like skin is almost as tough and impenetrable as an armor plate. But even though a dolphin's head is diminutive compared to the hammerhead's, what's going on inside of it is obviously better. Though sharks often gather in groups to feed, they fight individually. Dolphins, on the other hand, work together. They will surround a shark and take turns butting it until they are exhausted. And even if the sharks outnumber the school of dolphins, they will never imitate the group effort. Eventually they will get the message and swim away.

✦ *WHILE IT IS SWIMMING, A HAMMERHEAD DETECTS ELECTRICAL IMPULSES FROM OTHER CREATURES THAT ARE HIDING TO KEEP FROM BECOMING ITS NEXT MEAL.* ✦

ANIMALS OF THE AIR, ANIMALS OF THE WATER

The Taste
✦ OF ✦
New England

Ask any American to define the perfect meal and most will give you a one-word answer: lobster. There are dozens of species of lobsters in all parts of the world, but the one that comes to mind first is the one that comes from the cold waters off the Atlantic coast of New England and Canada, the one scientists call *Homarus Americanus*. It has a very close relative in northern Europe that the English call a lobster, the Germans a *hummer*, and the French *homard*. There is very little difference between the American and European versions, except for their color, but even tourists who think everything about Europe is just naturally better can't help pointing out that the *homard* is a poor excuse for a lobster dinner.

Actually, it would take a well-educated palate to tell the difference, and though Americans eat the New England type by the thousands, they haven't been at it long enough to make it a tradition. When Europeans first arrived in North America they found lobsters by the hundreds cluttering their beaches. Farmers used them for fertilizer, but the only human consumption was by the poor and servants of the upper classes. Eventually

✦ *LOBSTERS FROM THE NORTHEASTERN COASTLINE OF AMERICA ARE A GOURMET'S DELIGHT. BUT NOT ALL LOBSTERS ARE FROM THE ATLANTIC. THIS ONE (RIGHT) GREW UP ON THE PACIFIC COAST.* ✦

word got around that a lobster could be a tasty feast, and in about 1850 Maine fishermen began setting traps for them. Twenty years later, the Canadians began harvesting them, too, but nearly all of their catch was shipped to the United States. Not much more than a century later, when it became possible to ship them greater distances, environmentalists began wondering if *H. Americanus* might be in danger of extinction. The catch is getting smaller every year and the size of the lobsters caught is getting smaller, too.

The size of a lobster has very little to do with its age. Its rate of growth depends on water temperature, salinity, and the availability of food. Growth can also be slowed if the lobster has been in a fight. Like many kinds of lizards and starfish, they are able to lose a claw, an antenna, or a leg and grow a new one. But when they do regenerate, it is always at the expense of their own growth. In fact, in order to grow at all, lobsters need to shed their shells periodically. It takes two complete molting cycles to rebuild a missing limb, dur-

◆ THIS LOBSTER PREFERS THE WARM WATERS OF THE CARIBBEAN TO THE FRIGID HOMES OF ITS COUSINS. ◆

ing which time its body weight grows at a slower than normal rate, making for a smaller lobster.

The lobster's claws are not identical. The one on the left is larger but with a shorter grip, giving the lobster more power for crushing, and the one on the right is designed for ripping. The crusher claw can easily break a human finger. The lobster's tail is also powerful enough to cut a deep gash in any hand that gets too close. When it locates a meal, the big left claw breaks open the shell, and the other one tears at the meat inside. The pincers on its walking legs move the morsels toward its mouth, and the appendages known as maxillipeds at each side of the mouth hold the food in place while the mouth itself gets on with the business of getting it into the lobster's body. It is possibly the most inefficient feeding process in all of nature and most of

the food is carried away by the surrounding water, which is a boon to passing fish.

Lobsters are night hunters, using their long antennae to sense chemical changes in the water that announce the presence of a crab, a clam, a snail, a mussel, or a starfish, all of which, along with some fish and seaweed, constitute the lobster's diet. The antennae also provide a warning system should the lobster's archenemy, the codfish, happen to swim into its territory.

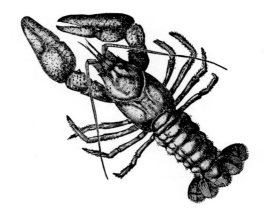

✦ ZAP! ✦

In a James Bond movie, 007 manages to surprise one of his attackers by sending him over a rail into an aquarium marked Danger! Electric Eel. The camera didn't record whether or not the current killed the man, but with an electrical charge of 500 volts, the six-foot-long creature that is normally at home in the fresh waters of the Amazon and Orinoco rivers could easily stop him in his tracks.

There are several hundred kinds of fish capable of generating electrical charges, but the electric eel of South America and Africa's electric catfish are the only freshwater species that, like torpedo rays and skates of the tropical oceans, are capable of producing enough voltage to light up a house.

The electricity-producing organs lie beneath the eel's skin extending forward from its tail. Each of them is made up of a series of disk-shaped electroplates all facing forward and stacked together like a roll of quarters and connected together in a series. A few are connected in parallel, which generates about one ampere of electricity, hardly enough to make the eel's electrical output useful except, of course, to the eel itself. The side facing the tail gives off a positive electrical charge and the other a negative charge, similar to the plus and minus terminals of a car battery. The water conducts the power to create a pulsating electrical field that surrounds the eel's body. Explorers have reported that some muddy backwaters of the South American rivers are often alive with electricity and that it is possible to hear the zapping of the discharges in them.

The question, of course, is why. Electric eels and other electricity-producing fishes generally live in muddy waters where the creatures they eat are usually hard to see. If that weren't enough, they also have what comes close to being the poorest eyesight in the marine world. But with the electrical field acting as a kind of radar device, the eels are easily able to detect a nearby meal. The eel also uses its electrical charge to stun other fish so that it can enjoy its meal in relative leisure with a minimum of fighting, which has given them a reputation of unusual laziness. In fact, it seems to turn up the voltage only when a small fish swims near. Electric eels are able to navigate themselves past underwater obstacles, often swimming backward. When using its electric organs for navigation, the charge is considerably weaker. Some observers think that the electrical impulses are also handy mating devices, allowing the eel to easily find a mate by detecting its similar electrical field.

Of all the species of electricity-producing fishes, the eel is the only one capable of varying its output.

✦ *ELECTRIC EELS STUN THEIR PREY WITH HIGH VOLTAGE, BUT THE POWER IS ALSO USEFUL TO THEM IN SOME OTHER WAYS.* ✦

ANIMALS OF THE AIR, ANIMALS OF THE WATER

✦ ROLE REVERSAL ✦

One of the basic laws of nature is that it is the responsibility of the female of any species to produce the young, to protect them when they are defenseless, and to prepare them to survive on their own. Different creatures handle the task in different ways, but in the case of the sea horse, the female seems to have better things to do than give birth and nurture babies. Those jobs are turned over to males of the species.

It is a big job. Within a day or two of delivering a brood of babies into the water, the male sea horse receives more eggs from the female and the process starts all over again. In his short life of about a year, he will deliver as many as nine different broods of some fifty babies each, and during the two months it takes them to grow to maturity, he takes on the responsibility of keeping them out of harm's way.

During mating, the female sea horse passes her eggs to the male and they are housed in an enclosed pouch under his tail, where they

will be fertilized. It isn't uncommon for a single male to accept the eggs of several females if his pouch is large enough. Once the eggs are fertilized, the male secretes enzymes to feed the growing embryos and in about three weeks they will be ready to emerge. Their father helps them by flexing his body. The babies are exact replicas of their parents and are fully equipped to get on with their own lives, and as if to prove it, they immediately swim to the surface for a gulp of air to fill their swim bladder and give them buoyancy. But they are tiny and easy prey for hungry fish and always swim back to their father, who in times of severe danger will allow them back into his pouch.

Instead of a tail fin, the sea horse has a coiling prehensile tail that it can wrap around the stems of plants to keep from being swept to places it doesn't want to go and to help it conceal itself in the junglelike underwater world of seaweed and grasses. It often stays in the same position for long periods of time, feeding on plankton, which it sucks from the surrounding water through its pipelike snout. But plankton don't always stay around waiting to be eaten, and when the little organisms are on the move, they manage to swim in a devious, elusive path. It requires some swimming skill on the part of the sea horse to catch them, even though the plankton move slowly. To accomplish its remarkable maneuverability, the sea horse wiggles its dorsal and pectoral fins from side to side in a flickering pattern that beats against the water and propels it. The fins move fast, but the sea horse doesn't. It doesn't have to. What it needs is the ability to perform fast turns and to be able to move upward and downward quickly, and the motion of its fins is perfect for both jobs.

✦ OPPOSITE PAGE: *THE SEAHORSE GRASPS THE STEMS OF PLANTS WITH ITS TAIL TO KEEP FROM BEING SWEPT ALONG BY THE CURRENT.* ✦

✦ *SEAHORSES OFTEN STAY ATTACHED TO PLANTS FOR HOURS, SUCKING PASSING PLANKTON THROUGH THEIR PIPELIKE SNOUT.* ✦

ANIMALS OF THE AIR, ANIMALS OF THE WATER

Of all the creatures that can kill a human, one of the deadliest is a lazy little foot-long fish that spends nearly all of its time lying among the rubble near the shores of the South Pacific and Indian oceans. It is usually hard to see because it lies so still for so long it is often covered with the same algae that coats the rocks and coral. But anyone unfortunate enough to touch a stonefish is usually dead within hours.

The stonefish is a member of the family of venomous scorpion fish, some of whom are the most beautiful sea creatures ever discovered. But all the beauty seems to have been bestowed on other members of the family. The stonefish is as ugly as it is lethal. It has a grotesque head that resembles a bulldog, and warty, slimy, dull-colored skin. Its back and sides are covered with spearlike spines encased in thick sheaths. It looks like one of the stones it lies among, one of the most perfect examples of camouflage in all of nature.

◆ *THE STONEFISH IS ALMOST IMPOSSIBLE TO SEE AMONG THE ROCKS ALONG THE SHORE, BUT ANYONE WHO TOUCHES ONE IS DOOMED TO ALMOST CERTAIN DEATH.* ◆

© Dave B. Fleetham/Tom Stack & Associates

And because of its disguise, the stonefish's prey almost never notices it is there until the predator's gaping mouth opens wide and there is no escape.

In most creatures, the camouflage would be enough. The stonefish doesn't seem to need its venom-filled spines either for protection or for hunting. Whether it needs it or not, the stonefish has developed the most sophisticated venom-producing system of all the poisonous fishes. It is even more efficient than most poisonous snakes. Nearly all of the

© Dave B. Fleetham/Tom Stack & Associates

scorpion fish produce their poison in grooves along the spines that jut out from their bodies like porcupine quills. When a victim gets too close, the venom flows along the groove. But the stonefish's spines have more efficient ducts inside them that work like hypodermic needles, and to add to its killing power, the spines are thicker and there are more of them. In one laboratory experiment, it was determined that a stonefish has enough venom to kill 36,000 mice and, of course, at least one human.

There is an antidote for the poison, but it isn't generally available except in well-equipped hospitals. Victims of a stonefish sting who can get to the hospital in time, though spared death, aren't spared the pain, which is said to be unbearable. South Pacific natives claim that people among them who have inadvertently stepped on a stonefish have been known to put their feet into a fire to try to stop the pain. None of them has even known anyone to have touched a stonefish and lived more than an hour before dying.

✦ *THE STONEFISH'S VENOM IS MORE DEADLY THAN MOST POISONOUS SNAKES. IT CARRIES ENOUGH POISON TO KILL 36,000 MICE.* ✦

✦ *TUBE SPONGES ARE AMONG THE*

CREATURES POPULATING AUSTRALIA'S

GREAT BARRIER REEF. ✦

◆ Bath Mate ◆

What could be more luxurious than a hot bath and a soft sponge to stroke away the cares of the day? These days, that sponge is more likely to be made from synthetic fibers than it is from an actual sea creature, but from the days of the ancient Greeks, sponges have been harvested from the sea and dried in the sun until nothing was left but the soft skeleton, which was then used for bathing and as padding.

Overfishing and a fungus that appeared in the 1930s wiped out most of the sponge beds that had been yielding some 2 million tons a year. Science hasn't been able to produce anything quite like the real thing.

Sponges had been growing on sea bottoms for more than half a billion years before man joined the animal kingdom. But it wasn't until a little more than a century ago that men finally made up their mind whether it was an animal or a vegetable. It is an animal but, like a plant, it doesn't have any means of moving around. And to compound the confusion, it doesn't have a mouth of any description and no apparent way of catching food.

Actually, the sponge is one of the pioneers in the evolution of one-celled animals into more specialized many-celled creatures, and it retains some of the characteristics of its ancestors. Like them, it draws nourishment solely from the water it lives in. It sucks water into its body through tiny pores on its surface and as the stream passes through, it draws organisms and oxygen out of it before it escapes through larger holes. This is a continuous process and it has been estimated that it takes a ton of water to provide the

sponge with enough microscopic plants and animals to equal a single ounce of weight. No matter how big it gets, the sponge can't digest anything larger than a single cell, a fact that makes it especially vulnerable to pollution and sediment. But it is able to protect itself because of an ability to contract the pores that bring life-giving water into its body, though the flow can't be stopped for long. To a sponge, it is the same thing as holding its breath.

In its natural environment, the type of sponge that might find its way into the bath is black and leathery; when it is cut open, the inside looks like raw beef liver. The millions of tiny pores that draw water into it are virtually invisible, but it is easy to see the larger holes that eject the water and to trace the channels inside that route it past the cells that extract the nutrients. When it is dried, nothing will remain except the large external vents and the skeleton that has supported the intricate network of internal canals.

◆ *SPONGES DRAW FOOD-RICH WATER INTO THEIR BODIES THROUGH TINY PORES AND EXPEL IT THROUGH LARGER HOLES.* ◆

ANIMALS OF THE AIR, ANIMALS OF THE WATER

✦ THE PRISONER ✦

As soon as a barnacle is born it is able to swim around in search of food. A few weeks into its life it picks a likely solid object and attaches itself to the object by appendages growing out of its head. At that point in its growth, it stops feeding and concentrates on surrounding itself with a hard, limelike shell. The shell itself is composed of several separate pieces that can be moved, but once it has been completely constructed, the barnacle inside can't move anywhere and has become trapped inside this prison of its own making.

It will spend the rest of its life standing on its head, fastened tightly to the surface it has chosen for its permanent residence and relying on its feet to get food inside. The feet extend out from under the shell and trap small organisms similar to the way a fisherman's net catches fish. Reducing its world to the inside of a cramped shell also limits the barnacle's reproductive life. It can't get outside to find a mate, but because they have a tendency to settle in colonies, there is usually another barnacle nearby. Since all barnacles combine male and female characteristics, there isn't any gender problem to get in the way of reproduction.

People who make their living from the sea usually regard barnacles as a nuisance because they attach themselves to wharves and pilings, and when they cover the bottoms of ships they create a drag on the hull that slows the ship down. They also have the nasty habit of fouling the blades of water-driven electrical turbines. They are usually the type known as gooseneck barnacles, which hang on by a leathery appendage that allows the creature inside the shell to get closer to the surrounding water. The acorn barnacle and others that cling to rocks fasten themselves more closely to the surface.

✦ BARNACLES NEVER COME OUT OF THEIR SHELLS, BUT EXTEND THEIR FEET OUTWARD TO TRAP FOOD. ✦

Both varieties are also often found clinging by the thousands to the skin of whales. But the whale is host to a third type that isn't found anywhere else. The so-called rabbit-eared barnacle has developed a pair of hoods above their shells to protect their feet when they are trapping food. They always cling with the hood openings facing forward in the direction the whale is swimming.

The whale, of course, is hardly aware of the barnacles on its back. But there are barnacles classed as "root headed" that make their home on the backs of crabs. And the host is very much aware of their presence. When it first attaches itself to the crab's back,

even before beginning to build its shell, the barnacle bores a hole into the crab's body and injects some of its own cells into the crab's bloodstream. They grow like a cancer and in time invade the crab's reproductive system. This not only makes the crab sterile, but transfers its hormones so that when it molts it will assume the body of a female, even if it has been a male to begin with. In the female form, the crab has a wider abdomen, which gives more protection to the barnacle. But protection isn't what the barnacle had in mind. It cuts a gash in the crab's abdomen and lays eggs inside. In time, the eggs will develop into early-stage barnacles.

✦ *GOOSENECK BARNACLES ATTACH THEMSELVES TO UNDERWATER SURFACES WITH AN APPENDAGE THAT ALLOWS THEM LIMITED MOVEMENT.* ✦

ANIMALS OF THE AIR, ANIMALS OF THE WATER

✦ CHAPTER THREE ✦

REPTILES
AND INSECTS

The Land
✦ of the ✦
Dragons

In 1912, a small plane crashed on the Indonesian island of Komodo, east of Java. The island was populated by prisoners exiled there by a local raja, few of whom had ever seen an airplane before, but all of whom swore they had seen dragons. By the time the pilot was rescued, he had seen them, too.

He said that their favorite food was wild pigs and goats and that he had even seen one devour a large deer. He hadn't seen one attack a man, but the natives had told him it happened every now and then, and that anyone unfortunate enough to get in a dragon's path never lived to tell the tale. But the pilot's own tales of the dragons of Komodo kept newspaper feature writers busy for months. With each new story, the creatures got bigger and more ferocious, even to the point of breathing fire.

Finally, a scientific expedition was dispatched to the island and came back with a photograph of one. But though it looked fierce, it was only seven feet long. In an attempt to confirm reports that the monsters averaged twenty feet, a big game hunter was sent in, but the best he could do was to capture four live specimens, all under ten feet. This was enough to confirm that the dragon was real, but that it was actually a giant monitor lizard, not a dragon, big enough to be in a class by itself and to be known ever since as the Komodo dragon.

Komodo dragons are very nearly the biggest land carnivores in the world, though the biggest specimen ever recorded was just slightly more than ten feet long and weighed 365 pounds. Because of the dragon's massive bulk, it isn't a tree climber as smaller lizards often are, but it moves quickly over land with its head in the air and its body high off the ground. It spends most of the day escaping the tropical heat in burrows or among thick jungle vegetation, hunting only in the early morning and late afternoon. All of them are

✦ *THIS FEMALE KOMODO DRAGON IS NEARLY SIX FEET LONG. HER MATE IS PROBABLY BIGGER.* ✦

© Nancy Adams/Tom Stack & Associates

good swimmers, and some even cross short stretches of the sea to offshore islands in search of game or eggs, which are their favorite food.

Komodo dragons hunt like cats, hiding in underbrush and ambushing their prey. They move quickly, grabbing the animal by the throat with their sharklike teeth and then completely devouring it. A fifty-pound pig can vanish without a trace in fifteen minutes; a thousand-pound water buffalo takes a little longer. In their island world, the giant lizards have no enemies, only victims. But when they feel threatened, they puff up their chest and give a warning hiss. If that doesn't remove the threat, showing their sharp teeth and

claws usually does the trick. Smaller monitors lash out with their tails, which prove to be an effective weapon, but the Komodo dragon doesn't seem to use its tail as a scare tactic.

As it turns out, the early reports of attacks on man weren't exaggerated. When scientists discovered that the Komodo dragon was actually a monitor, they reassured the world that it was safe to walk among them because unprovoked monitors avoid human contact. On the island of Komodo, however, things are different. The dragon is the king of the beasts there, and though it doesn't seem to consider human flesh a delicacy, it will attack a man, often for no reason at all, except possibly pure meanness.

◆ *KOMODO DRAGONS ARE THE UNDISPUTED KINGS OF THEIR SOUTH PACIFIC JUNGLE HOME, WHERE THEY HAVE ELIMINATED THEIR NATURAL ENEMIES.* ◆

THE LIZARD
✦ THAT WALKS ON ✦
WATER

In ancient mythology, the basilisk was considered the most deadly creature of all. Allegedly hatched from a hen's egg by a toad, it possessed the body of a snake and the head of a rooster. Its foul breath had the same effect as a poison gas, powerful enough to kill any animal, and it was said that just looking it in the eye would result in instant death.

Among its identifying marks was a crest on its forehead with a mark that looked like a crown. And it was a similar crest that early

explorers in the Central American forest noticed when they came upon a three-foot-long lizard with a very long tail they were certain must be that foul-smelling serpent with the evil eye, known to them as the basilisk. Naturally, they didn't stay around it long enough to confirm their suspicions, but even when it turned out to be nothing more than a harmless little lizard, the name stuck.

The basilisk didn't stay around to observe the explorers, either. As it always does when it feels threatened, it raised itself up on its hind legs and began running. Using its tail for balance, it can run great distances on two legs. Such things aren't unique in the animal kingdom. Iguanas, the basilisk's relatives, often run on two legs, but the basilisk has a related talent that is more unusual. When it

◆ *THE BASILISK'S NAME COMES FROM A HORRIBLE MYTHICAL MONSTER, BUT ITS APPEARANCE DOESN'T LIVE UP TO ITS ANCIENT REPUTATION.* ◆

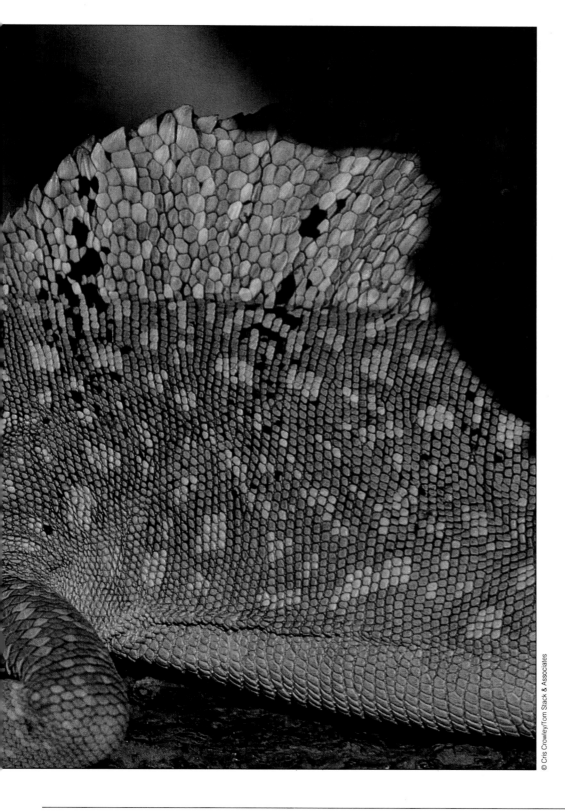

© Cris Crowley/Tom Stack & Associates

REPTILES AND INSECTS

✦ *THE MYTHICAL BASILISK WAS DREADED BECAUSE OF ITS EVIL EYE, BUT A GLANCE FROM A REAL ONE CAN'T HARM YOU.* ✦

comes to a body of water, it just keeps on going. Its big feet and light body allow it to run as far as a quarter of a mile on the surface of the water. The trick is that the basilisk has to keep running. If it loses speed it will sink, but it is a good swimmer, although it prefers to be on the water, not under it. The basilisk has a Cuban cousin called the Deiroptyx that shares their water-walking ability, but it runs short distances and then dives for safety.

The crest on the basilisk's head is raised and its lower jaw puffs up when it is feeling angry or threatened. However, contrary to the old stories, its breath isn't fatal to man or beast. On the other hand, the display is

surely intended to frighten away any intruder to its territory. If the trick doesn't work, the basilisk rises up on its hind legs and gets out of harm's way as fast as its little legs can carry it.

Lizards nearly always search for food in the daytime, when insects are plentiful and they can see the succulent plant leaves and flowers. But one of the 3,000 different types of them, the gecko breaks all the rules. It thrives in the desert, and it does all of its hunting at night. Its skin, thin enough to see through to its internal organs, isn't scaly like a lizard's and its tail is fatter than the rest of its body. At least one variety that lives in Java has an expandable membrane on the side of its body that acts like a sail and allows it to soar through the air. All geckos move very slowly and deliberately and regularly engage in feeding frenzies for a couple of days, storing up enough sustenance to last as long as six months.

The gecko's tail is one of the strangest features of any creature in the world. When it feels threatened and decides to run away from danger, it will detach its tail and leave it behind as a decoy. It's a great sacrifice on the part of the gecko. It will grow a new one in a

✦ *THE GECKO IS A MEMBER OF THE LIZARD FAMILY, BUT NO OTHER LIZARD IS QUITE LIKE IT.* ✦

✦ *BECAUSE IT HAS NO EYELIDS, THE*

GECKO SEEMS TO BE FOREVER STARING. ✦

few days, but because it uses its tail to store the fat that carries it through to the next meal, it needs to keep eating until the tail is replaced.

But as if all that weren't unusual enough, the gecko also has what may be the strangest eyes in the animal kingdom. There is no bony structure around them and light passes through them to create the impression that the gecko has a hole in its head when it is seen in front of a bright light. The gecko doesn't have eyelids and usually gives the impression of staring in disbelief, but it controls the amount of light entering it with slits in the pupils, very much like cats' eyes. Even when the slits are closed, the gecko can still see. The slits have a series of tiny notches along their sides, and even when the pupils are closed, light enters through them. None of the holes is big enough to allow in enough light to form an image, but the light that

passes through several of them is all focused together on the retina to form a sharp picture. Because of the tiny pinholes in the pupils of its eye, the gecko is able go outdoors in full sunlight without harming its ability to see in near darkness.

Geckos are frequently kept as house pets because of their appetite for insects. In Burma there isn't a temple or monastery that doesn't have at least one, and the Buddhist monks routinely spend their evenings listening for its unpredictable loud call.

✦ *THE GECKO'S TAIL IS FREQUENTLY CHEWED OFF IN FIGHTS, BUT IT ALWAYS GROWS BACK.* ✦

✦ *THE GECKO IS SO THIN-SKINNED, IT IS NEARLY TRANSPARENT.* ✦

A Snake
✦ with ✦
Legs

There are nearly three thousand different lizards in the world but only five or six species that grow to be more than five feet long. These few big lizards became known as monitors after a German zoologist mistranslated an Arabic name for them, which became in his language "warning lizard." English scientists picked up the signal and gave the creature a name close in meaning, although it is rare that a monitor gives a warning of its presence.

Most scientists agree that monitors have been roaming the earth for about 80 million years and that until about a million years ago, they were about twenty feet long. Today, ten feet is considered long for a monitor, and some varieties are only about a foot long. Zoologists also agree that they are more closely related to snakes than to other lizards and that both probably emerged from the same prehistoric creatures. For evidence they

point to the monitor's forked tongue, which is identical to a snake's and is used in the same way. It picks up particles in the air and transports them to a sensor in the roof of its mouth, where a chemical reaction allows it to identify the presence of danger or its next meal.

Nearly all monitors live in Australia, New Guinea, and Indonesia. Others thrive in India and Pakistan and in Egypt along the Nile River. Among the Australian varieties, the one they call the giant goanna averages eight feet long. It is only slightly larger than the lace monitor, a tree lizard named for the yellow lacy pattern on its black skin. Most monitors are good climbers and nearly all of them can outrun any creature that might have the temerity to threaten them. Monitors are good swimmers, too, capable of propelling themselves through the water with their tails in the same way crocodiles are able to. They are also able to stay underwater for long periods of time, and in some human settlements they frequently choose to live inside wells. When running they look almost ludicrous, but their waddling gait is deceptive. Over short stretches, all monitors are easily able to outrun a man.

Many types of monitors have developed the habit of laying their eggs in termite nests. The wood-eating insects provide just the right temperature for hatching lizard eggs and the babies come into the world in the midst of a handy food supply. Monitor youngsters are among the most attractive of all lizards, with intricate patterns traced on a skin that looks like beadwork. As they grow older, the colors deepen and many of the spots in the texture disappear. They grow about an inch every month and reach their full size in less than three years.

✦ *MONITORS ARE THE GIANTS OF THE LIZARD FAMILY AND, IN THE OPINION OF SOME, THE MOST BEAUTIFUL.* ✦

Monitors are exclusively meat eaters, and no creature from a cockroach to a squirrel is safe from them. The larger they get, the larger their prey becomes. In some places they are the scourge of poultry farmers. They all have a taste for fresh eggs, and if a hen happens to be sitting on them, she becomes part of the meal, too.

✦ *THE AUSTRALIAN LACE MONITOR* (BELOW) *IS AN ACCOMPLISHED TREE-CLIMBER. ALL MONITOR VARIETIES HAVE SNAKELIKE FORKED TONGUES* (LEFT). ✦

REPTILES AND INSECTS

◆ FASHION PLATE ◆

The American branch of a chameleon family is known in the Deep South as the green lizard, but it isn't always green. Most of the time it is usually brown or dark gray, but like all chameleons, it changes color as routinely as a fashion model changes clothes.

At one time, it was possible to buy chameleons at carnivals and novelty stores to be worn like jewelry that adapts its color to match the rest of your outfit. Fortunately for the chameleons, it isn't done any more, possibly because the trick didn't work. The little lizard was as likely to be brown on a green blouse as it was to be green on a red one. The ability to change color seems to have nothing to do with blending into the background.

When it is asleep, a chameleon is usually pale green and its underside is white. When it is fighting it displays the same colors, but as the pressure of the fight builds, the green turns brighter and extends to the underside. When it is sitting in the sun, it will usually turn dark brown, but as the sun fades, the chameleon's skin fades to a soft yellow. The color changes take place quickly, usually in about two or three minutes, and seem to be determined by such things as temperature and light as well as anger or fear.

People who once bought chameleons as fashion items may have been disappointed by their range of colors, but they often discovered another advantage to have a chameleon around the house. They have voracious appetites and are especially fond of houseflies and mosquitoes. As it stalks them, it is capable of scurrying up walls and across ceilings because it has little adhesive pads on its feet. Chameleons hunt insects very much in the same way cats hunt birds. Once it finds its prey, it slinks forward, low to the surface,

◆ *THE EAST AFRICAN JACKSON'S CHAMELEON IS MORE MENACING-LOOKING THAN ITS AMERICAN COUSINS.* ◆

✦ *THE LEOPARD LIZARD* (LEFT) *IS AT HOME IN THE DESERTS OF THE AMERICAN SOUTHWEST.* ✦

✦ *STALKING INSECT PREY* (LEFT) *IS THE LEOPARD LIZARD'S FAVORITE SPORT.* ✦

then it quivers for an instant and pounces. It eats small insects whole, but seems to take pleasure in chewing up the bigger ones.

Chameleons are better than average hunters because of their unusual eyes, which are set in little bumps on the top of its head. Each of them is independent of the other, and as a chameleon is stalking a tasty moth or a mosquito with one eye, the other one is on the lookout for the next course.

When two chameleons fight each other the battle isn't considered over until one of them has bitten off the tail of the other and marched off in triumph with the trophy in its mouth. Like most other lizards, the loser of the tail is able to grow a new one in a very short time, but it will always have a bump to mark the spot where the new growth began, serving as a reminder of that fateful day.

REPTILES AND INSECTS

"The Ugliest ✦ Creatures in ✦ Nature"

Back in the days when pirates sailed the seas, one of them described the giant land tortoises of the Galapagos Islands as the ugliest of all creatures. "They look very old and bleak," he said. It's probably because many of them are. No one knows for sure quite how old they live to be, but one that died—in an accident, mind you—in 1918 had been kept as a military mascot for 152 years and it was already full grown when it became a pet. Full grown for a Galapagos tortoise means a length of five or six feet and a weight of as much as six hundred pounds. They weigh less than a pound when they hatch, but their weight more than doubles each year.

Charles Darwin, the first scientist to observe Galapagos tortoises, clocked their average speed at 360 yards an hour and said that, allowing time to eat along the road, they could cover as much as four miles in a day.

He noticed that they seemed to require large amounts of water and because the only source was at the top of steep hills, most of the tortoises were either plodding uphill for a drink or heading back down to feed on prickly pears and cactus. When they reach fresh water they completely submerge their heads, wallowing with great, gasping gulps for several minutes before resting for the torturous trip back down the hill. They invariably follow the same routes and have worn smooth paths in the lavalike rock between feeding grounds and watering holes.

The combination of steady habits and a slow pace makes the giant tortoise quite easy to catch. Though they are well protected inside their thick shells, they are no match for man, who has been bent on their destruction for hundreds of years. The earliest sailing ships made these islands six hundred miles off the coast of present-day Ecuador a regular port of call, as did the warships that followed them and the whalers who came later. In every case, the tortoise was the reason. As one old pirate said, "They are extraordinarily large and fat and so sweet

✦ *IT TAKES ALL DAY FOR A GALAPAGOS TORTOISE TO COVER A DISTANCE OF FOUR MILES.* ✦

✦ *IF A HAWK ISN'T IN MUCH OF A HURRY, THE TORTOISE DOESN'T MIND IF IT HITCHES A RIDE.* ✦

that no pullet eats more pleasantly.'' After months at sea living on rock-hard dried beef, the tortoises must have seemed like manna from heaven. But more than a source of fresh meat, the tortoise also provided an oil that seafarers said was better than fresh butter. One whaling captain who stopped at the Galapagos after rounding the Horn wrote that he had taken several hundred tortoises, enough to provision his vessel for as long as six months. Sailors before him had discovered that it was possible for the creatures to live as long as fourteen months without food or water and that the only care they required was to make sure their shells didn't get broken.

The slaughter slowed in the early years of the twentieth century, but by then the tortoises had completely disappeared from five of the eighteen islands in the archipelago. Then the scientists moved in. As one expedition after another took specimens for study, they declared some of the varying species

extinct. If others happened to find what appeared to be survivors, they were either removed for ''protection'' or killed for study. Today all varieties of Galapagos tortoises are under the protection of the Ecuadorian government, and those that remain are struggling toward a secure future. Slowly, of course.

✦ *COLONIES OF GALAPAGOS TORTOISES PROVIDED EARLY SAILORS WITH A HANDY SOURCE OF FOOD.* ✦

REPTILES AND INSECTS

PRAYING
✦ OR ✦
PREYING?

In Moslem countries it is widely believed that the insect called a praying mantis is always facing Mecca and always holding its forelegs in an attitude of prayer. The word *mantis*, in fact, comes from a Greek word meaning ''prophet.'' Obviously, this close relative of the grasshopper and the cockroach got its name because it looks like it is praying; it holds its front legs in a position close to its mouth. Actually, in this position the mantis is preying, and any insect that comes within reach becomes the mantis' next meal with a minimum of movement.

The mantis always moves slowly, almost imperceptibly, so that its position won't be discovered until it is too late. When an unsuspecting creature gets too near, the mantis lashes out with its grasping, spiny legs and begins pulling it apart, devouring it in sec-

onds. It never seems to get full and will eat anything that happens along, even another mantis, which makes mating a tricky business.

In tropical countries these insects grow much larger than the ones commonly found in the United States, and many varieties have evolved into creatures that look like plants. Some have leaflike extensions from their sides, others look like flowers. Among those, they have developed a habit of hanging from branches and swaying slightly to heighten the illusion. It is the only variety that moves while searching for food, although some others will stalk for short distances when the pickings seem slim. Still other varieties have altered their appearance over time to look like other insects and routinely make banquets of colonies of them.

Most praying mantises are exclusively insect eaters, but in the South American jungles, where the mantises are often giants, they eat small birds and lizards. The only rule that seems to govern their taste in prey is size. To a praying mantis, anything that is smaller than itself is edible. Except for that, the only rule that governs a mantis's existence is patient waiting. Sooner or later, something tasty is sure to come along. About the only creature that outdoes a mantis for patience is a tiny wasp that sometimes attaches itself to the mantis's back at a spot between the wings, where neither jaws nor feet can reach it. It waits for the larger insect to lay its eggs on a twig, and before the mantis can cover them with the frothy substance that hardens and protects them, the wasp lays her own eggs on the cluster. As larvae, the wasps will live on the mantis eggs, protected from the outside world by the shell the adult mantis has provided.

✦ *PRAYING MANTISES HATCH FROM EGGS PROTECTED IN A HARD-SHELLED CASE BUILT BY THE FEMALE.* ✦

◆ *THE MANTIS'S EYES ARE POWERFUL ENOUGH TO ALLOW IT TO HUNT WHILE STANDING STILL (LEFT).* ◆

◆ *A YOUNG MANTIS LIVES ON TINY INSECTS (LEFT), BUT AS IT GETS BIGGER, SO DOES ITS PREY.* ◆

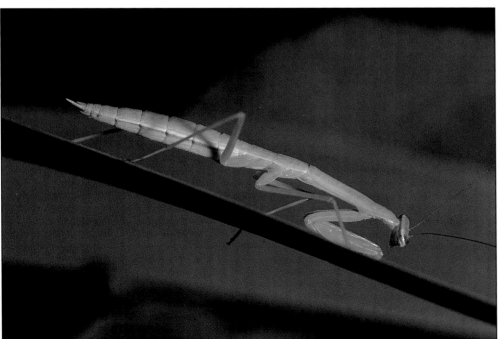

REPTILES AND INSECTS

◆ NATURE'S ◆ AIRPLANE

Men dreamed of flying like birds for thousands of years, but when they found a way, the airplane turned out to be more of an imitation of a dragonfly than a bird.

A dragonfly is capable of hovering, moving straight up, even flying backward. It can fly forward as fast as sixty miles an hour and its wings are strong enough to allow it to fly off, without sacrificing speed, with an insect heavier than itself clutched in its legs. The dragonfly rarely uses its six legs for walking; instead, it uses them to pluck other insects from the air and, still flying forward at breakneck speed, it uses its front legs to move the victim to its mouth. Once it has disappeared, the dragonfly is ready for another morsel. It is capable of consuming its own weight in less than a half hour.

Dragonflies are especially fond of mosquitoes, and sometimes catch so many of them that they can't close their mouths. They are always on the lookout for more, and even the tiniest mosquito can't escape them. The dragonfly has what may well be the sharpest eyes in nature. It can see in every direction at the same time and can spot a mosquito one hundred feet away. The eyes are made up of as many as 30,000 six-sided lenses massed together in a bulge that covers most of its head.

There are some 4,870 species of dragonflies, and though some migrate hundreds of miles to escape the chill of fall and winter, their flying lives are limited to a single season. The first frost usually kills off the existing population, but by then the females have deposited thousands of eggs, and when they hatch in the spring, they will emerge as creatures quite unlike their parents except for their insatiable hunger.

In the first stages of its life, the creature that emerges as a dragonfly will live underwater for at least a year and in some cases as long as five years, spending every moment stalking prey. Its lower jaw is constructed very much like an arm, even including an elbow joint. At its end are two sharp claws that can

◆ *A DRAGONFLY SPENDS NEARLY ALL OF ITS ADULT LIFE ON THE WING, AND CAN FLY AS FAST AS SIXTY MILES AN HOUR.* ◆

grasp anything that moves, and the immature dragonfly has a taste for anything that moves. When it gets close to a victim, the jaw lashes out, grabs the morsel, and swallows it in the twinkling of an eye. It moves through the mud on the bottom of ponds and streams on a leg that will become useless when it reaches the adult stage, but when it needs speed, it has a well-developed form of jet propulsion to rely on. It normally breathes through gills inside its body and the water that feeds them oxygen is rhythmically drawn in and expelled. When the creature wants a burst of speed, it expels the water with sudden force and moves like an underwater rocket. Their food is usually other immature insects and minnows, but they'll eat anything that moves, even other baby dragonflies.

During their days as the scourge of the bottom, they molt several times until finally they move up headfirst from the water for the final shedding of their protective shells. At this point, for the several hours it takes for the new insect's wings to be able to carry it off, the dragonfly is at the most vulnerable point of its life. If it should fall back into the water, where it has lived all those long months, it will drown.

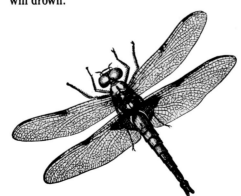

✦ *THE DRAGONFLY'S WINGS ALLOW IT TO CARRY OFF LARGER INSECTS WITHOUT SLOWING DOWN.* ✦

INDEX

A

Aardvarks

    burrowing ability of, 45

    claws, 45

    description of, 44

    solitary nature of, 44, 45

Alligators, in mythical inspiration, 10

Anemones

    anatomical simplicity, 77

    camouflage, 77

    flowerlike appearance of, 77

    habitat, 78

    longevity, 77–78

    reproduction, 78

Aristotle, 13, 82, 83

Armadillos

    armor covering on, 46–47

    defense behavior, 47

    habitat, 46

    species in the United States, 46

B

Barnacles

    as crab parasite, 97

    as maritime nuisance, 96

    shell of, 96

    whales and, 97

Basilisks

    defense behavior, 103, 104

    description and markings, 102–3

    mythologies concerning, 102

    water–running ability, 104

Bears. *See* Grizzly bears

Bible, leviathan myth in, 10

C

Caesar, Julius, 13

Chameleons

    coloring, 110

    diet, 110–11

    eyes, 111

    tail, 111

Columbus, Christopher, 41

Crabs, barnacles as parasites on, 97

Crocodiles, in mythical inspiration, 10

D

Darwin, Charles, 59, 112

David, Armand, 32, 35

Dingoes, as kangaroo enemies, 62

Dolphins, as enemies of

        hammerhead sharks, 85

Dragonflies

    anatomy, 116–17

    diet, 116

    flight ability and speed, 116

    life cycle, 116

    mobility, 117

Dragons, 10–11

Dugongs, manatees compared with, 43

E

Edgar, J.H., 32

Electric eels, electrical charge of, 89

Elizabeth I (England), 13

Emus

    as flightless bird, 72

    grazing habits, 72–73

    parenting by, 73

    personality traits, 73

    size, 72

G

Galapagos tortoises

    endangerment, 113

    humans as predators on, 112–13

    longevity, 112

    speed of, 112

Geckos

    description, 105

    eyes, 107

    as house pets, 107

    tail, 105–7

George, Saint, 10–11

Giraffes

    defense mechanisms, 24

    eyesight, 25

    group behavior, 24–25

    hunting of, 24

Griffin, 12

Grizzly bears

    brown bears compared with, 20

    character and nature of, 20–22

    hierarchy among, 22–23

    as weather forecasters, 23

H

Hammerhead sharks

    description and characteristics, 84

    dolphins as natural enemies of, 85

Poe, Edgar Allan, 59

Portuguese man-of-war

    anatomy, 74

    as coastal menace, 74

    sea turtles as enemy of, 74

Praying mantises

    description, 114

    diet, 114

    hunting by, 114

Proboscis monkeys

    face and body markings, 51–53

    nose, 51, 53

    social behavior of, 53

R

Rails

    description and behavior, 70

    habitat, 70

    number of species, 70

Rhinoceroses

    character and nature of, 18–19

    horns, 17

    as loners, 18

    oxpecker bird and, 18

S

Satyrs, 59

Seahorses

    mating and reproduction, 91

    plankton in diet of, 91

    tail, 91

Sea otters

    description, 38

    diet, 38

feeding behavior, 38–40

    fur, 40

    tool-using ability, 38

Sea turtles

    as enemy of Portuguese man-of-war, 74

Shrews

    diet, 50

    metabolism of, 50

    reputation of, 50

Sloths

    anatomy and metabolism rate, 28–29

    arboreal habitat, 28

    eating and diet, 29-30

    swimming ability, 30

    time spent sleeping, 28

Species, number and variety of, 9

Sponges

    description, 95

    endangerment, 95

    evolution and classification, 95

    nourishing method, 95

Starfish

    anatomy, 79

    coloring, 79

    feet, 81

    mobility, 79–81

    number of species, 79

Stingrays, as prey of hammerhead sharks, 84

Stonefish

    camouflage, 92–93

    deadliness of, 92–93

T

Tarsiers

    acrobatic ability of, 56

    description of, 56

    diet, 56

    difficulty in observing, 56

    lemurs related to, 56

    mating and offspring, 56

Tasmanian wolf

    endangerment of, 67

    as marsupial, 67

    mythologies surrounding, 67

    predatory nature of, 67

U

Unicorns

    on British coat of arms, 11

    early myths of, 12

    legends regarding, 12–13

    rhinoceroses and, 17

V

Vespucci, Amerigo, 27

W

Wallace, Alfred Russell, 59

Whales, barnacles and, 97